DEDICATION

Hi'ipoi i ka 'aina aloha
(Cherish the beloved land)

Aloha!

HIKING HAWAII

The Big Island

By Robert Smith

A Hawaiian Outdoor Adventures Publication

FIRST EDITION 1977
SECOND EDITION 1980
THIRD EDITION, OCTOBER 1989
FOURTH EDITION, JANUARY 1993
Copyright 1977, 1980, 1989, 1993 by Robert Smith

Maps by Kevin G. Chard
Typesetting by The Acacia Group
Cover photo by Diane G. Harper
Photos by author and Diane G. Harper

Library of Congress Card Catalog Card Number 79-93248
International Standard Book Number 0-924308-02-8

Manufactured in the United States
Published by Hawaiian Outdoor Adventures Publications

ACKNOWLEDGEMENTS

I am indebted to a number of people who generously offered their time and effort to make this book possible. Many thanks to the park rangers of the Hawaii Volcanoes National Park whose assistance and knowledge were invaluable. Thanks also to Cheryl Anne Litchie, who checked the manuscript and who typed it. I am indebted to Fred Samia who read the manuscript and offered valuable advice, and to Diane G. Harper, who contributed many of the photos in this book and who assisted me on many of the trails.

— Robert Smith
   Maui, Hawaii
   1993

BOOKS BY ROBERT SMITH

Hawaii's Best Hiking Trails

Hiking Maui, The Valley Isle

Hiking Oahu, The Capital Isle

Hiking Hawaii, The Big Island

Hiking Kauai, The Garden Isle

"DESTROYED BY LAVA" is a common sign seen on the Big Island. Kilauea Volcano has been erupting almost continuously since 1983 from the Puu O'o vent on the east side of the island. Lava has overrun and closed the "Kalapana Coastline" (Hiking Area #4) and the "Kamoamoa" hike and campground in Hawaii Volcanoes National Park. As of this date (January, 1993) Kilauea continues to erupt.

Every effort is made to provide our readers with information when permission is required to hike on private land. Some private landowners allow hiking without permission and then change their mind, or they withdraw permission without notice. *Please* respect "Kapu" ("No Trespassing") signs.

CONTENTS

Madame Pele's artwork!

Part I:

Introduction

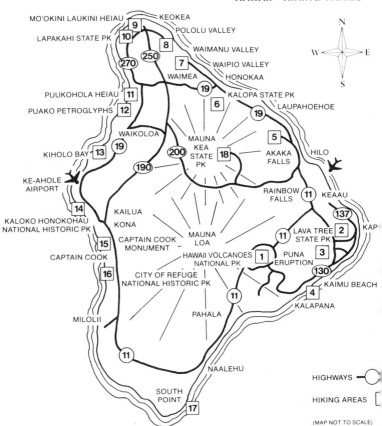

HAWAII—HIKING TRAILS

MO'OKINI LAUKINI HEIAU   KEOKEA

LAPAKAHI STATE PK   9   POLOLU VALLEY

10

270   250   8   WAIMANU VALLEY

7   WAIPIO VALLEY

WAIMEA   HONOKAA

19

PUUKOHOLA HEIAU   11   KALOPA STATE PK

PUAKO PETROGLYPHS   12   6   LAUPAHOEHOE

19

WAIKOLOA   5

MAUNA KEA STATE PK

KIHOLO BAY   13   19   200   18   AKAKA FALLS   HILO

190

KE-AHOLE AIRPORT   RAINBOW FALLS   11   KEAAU

137

14   KAILUA KONA   2   KAP

KALOKO HONOKOHAU NATIONAL HISTORIC PK   11   LAVA TREE STATE PK

15   CAPTAIN COOK MONUMENT   MAUNA LOA   3

CAPTAIN COOK   HAWAII VOLCANOES NATIONAL PK   1   PUNA ERUPTION

16   CITY OF REFUGE NATIONAL HISTORIC PK   130

KAIMU BEACH

4

MILOLII   PAHALA   11   KALAPANA

11

NAALEHU

SOUTH POINT   17

HIGHWAYS ⬤

HIKING AREAS

(MAP NOT TO SCALE)

THE ISLAND

"Here today, gone tomorrow" is applied or mis-applied to a variety of situations. It might well be the motto of the Island of Hawaii. Certainly no other island in the Hawaiian chain and perhaps no other place on earth experiences such dramatic and spectacular changes in such short periods of time. The "Big Island" - sometimes the "Orchid Island" or the "Volcano Island" -is the site of Mauna Loa, the world's largest active volcano and the largest single mountain on earth. In addition to Mauna Loa's frequent eruptions, another reason for all the change is the active shield volcano, Kilauea, in whose caldera Pele, the legendary and mischievous goddess of volcanoes, is said to reside. Kilauea, the "drive-in volcano," is a place where volcanic eruptions and lava flows can be viewed safely from an automobile or even more closely on foot. As of July, 1989, Kilauea had been erupting for 67 months along its southeast rift. It has been emitting an average of 650,00 cubic yards of lava daily.

With every eruption, the spewing lava alters the island in some way. Roads are overcome by the flowing lava, hiking trails are covered by ash or pumice, sometimes homes are destroyed, infrequently lives are lost, and, on occasion, new land is added to the state. For example, during an eruption in 1960, lava flowed into the sea and added 500 acres of land to the east side of the island. Thus, Hawaii was now 500 feet closer to California! And between 1987-89, successive eruptions from Kilauea closed the Chain of Craters Road (March, 1987), destroyed the Wahaula Visitor Center (June, 1989), overran and burned 71 homes, and presently (August, 1989) threatens Wahaula Heiau, a 700-yearold Hawaiian temple. Madame Pele is a very busy lady!

The largest (4,038 square miles) of the Hawaiian Islands, Hawaii was formed by the building of five volcanoes. In the north, the now-extinct Kohala volcano is the oldest, rising to 5,505 feet. Its peaks have been eroded to deep, precipitous valleys. Hualalai volcano (8,251 feet) in the west last erupted in 1801 and is considered dormant. Towering, majestic Mauna Kea volcano dominates central Hawaii and at 13,796 feet is the highest peak on the island. Snow and winter sports are popular on its slopes. The remaining two volcanoes command most of the attention because of frequent volcanic activity. Mauna Loa (13,680 feet) is the world's largest active volcano, and Kilauea, while a mere

4,077 feet, has been the site of the most recent eruptions on the island.

Hawaii is about the size of Connecticut, and nearly 5 times the size of any other island in the chain: 93 miles long, 76 miles wide and 318 miles around. One can drive completely around the island on good surfaced roads, a convenience not found on the other "neighbor" islands - Maui, Kauai, Molokai and Lanai.

Historically, Hawaii is believed to be the first island reached by Polynesian settlers, about 750 A.D. It is the birthplace of Kamehameha the Great, who conquered and unified the islands in the late 18th century. It is also the place where Captain James Cook was killed (1779) after he "discovered" (1778) the islands and introduced Western culture. However, perhaps the most notable resident is Pele, the goddess of volcanoes, who is said to reside in Halemaumau, Kilauea's fire pit.

Hiking and backpacking on the Big Island have increased in popularity in recent years. Backpacks are conspicuous at baggage counters as more and more visitors seek to discover a Hawaii different from the standard tourist fare. Trails here take you to enchanting black sand beaches, across the world's most active volcano, and to the highest peaks - Mauna Loa and Mauna Kea - over 13,000 feet in the 50th state.

USING THIS BOOK

Hiking on the Big Island is an exciting and sometimes spectacular experience because of periodic volcanic activity. Few will dispute that the best trails and the most memorable experiences are found in Hawaii Volcanoes National Park. However, some prefer the North Kohala Mountains, with their verdant and precipitous valleys. In any case, day hiking on Hawaii does not generally require any special equipment or skill. Many places of unique and extraordinary beauty are readily accessible to the novice, to the family, or to the elderly who are looking for short, relatively easy hikes or walks.

In planning a hike, the reader is advised to consult the Hiking Chart below in order to give due consideration to driving time, hiking time, and the clothing and supplies necessary. I have rated all the hikes and placed them in four categories. A family rated hike is for those who are looking for short, easy hikes. The hardy family classification requires a degree of effort and sound physical condition. Both the strenuous and the difficult hikes require a measure of endurance, since they are longer hikes and most of them involve a considerable gain in

Hiking Chart

HIKING AREA NUMBER

No.	Hiking Area	Family	Hardy family	Difficult	Strenuous	Distance (miles)	Time (hours)	Gain (feet)	Hilo Miles	Hilo Time (hours)	Kona Miles	Kona Time (hours)	Boots	Raingear	Take Food	Carry Water	Tennis Shoes OK	Swimming	Views	Waterfalls	Historical Sites	Fruits
1	Volcanoes National Park								30	1	95	2½										
	Mauna Loa Strip Rd.																					
	Kipuka Puaula	X				1.1	1						X	X	X							
	Mauna Loa Summit				X	19.6	3-4 Days	7015					X	X		X	X		X		X	
	Kilauea Caldera Area																					
	Crater Rim			X		11.6	5-8	500					X	X		X	X		X		X	
	Halemaumau	X				3.2	2							X		X	X		X		X	
	Byron Ledge			X		2.5	1½	200					X	X		X	X		X		X	
	Kilauea Iki			X		4.0	2½	400					X	X		X	X		X		X	
	Thurston Lava Tube	X				.3	1/4								X							X
	Devastation	X				.6	1/4								X				X			X
	Sandalwood	X				.7	1/4								X				X			X
	Sulphur Bank	X				.3	1/4								X						X	
	Kau Desert Area																					
	Halape				X	7.2	4	3000					X		X	X		X			X	X
	Hilina Pali			X		4.2	3	2000					X		X	X			X			
	Kau Desert				X	19.9	10	4000					X		X	X			X		X	
	Mauna Iki				X	8.8	5						X		X	X			X		X	
	Keauhou				X	8.0	8	2500					X		X	X			X			
	Kau-Puna				X	11.0	6						X		X	X		X			X	
	Kalpana Area																					
	~~Kamoamoa~~	X				1.0	1								X						X	X
	Puu Loa Petroglyphs		X			1.0	3/4								X						X	X
	Napau			X		7.0	4	400					X		X	X			X		X	
	Nauli		X			2.0	1	250					X		X	X			X			
	Kalapana			X		9.2	5	2500					X		X	X			X			
2	Lava Trees State Park	X				.8	1/2		24	3/4	130	3½			X							X
3	Puna Eruption	X				2.0	1		28	1	134	3½	X	X	X				X		X	
4	~~Kalapana Coastline~~	X				2.0	1		32	1	138	3½	X	X				X			X	X
5	Akaka Falls	X				.7	1/2		15	3/4	87	2½			X				X	X		
6	Kalopa State Park								42	1	61	1½										
	Nature Trail	X				.7	1						X	X	X							
	Kalopa Gulch Loop		X			2.8	2						X	X	X	X			X			X
7	Waipio/Waimanu Valleys								50	1½	65	2										
	Waipio			X		3.0	2	900					X	X		X	X	X	X	X	X	X
	Waimanu				X	9.0	7	1000					X	X		X	X	X	X	X	X	X
8	Pololu Valley			X		½	½	900	80	2	66	1	X	X		X	X	X	X	X		X
9	Mo'okini Laukini Heiau	X				1.0	1		81	2	52	1			X						X	X
10	Lapakahi State Park	X				1.5	1		80	2	47	1			X			X			X	X
11	Puukohola Heiau		X			1.0	1		63	1½	35	1	X	X				X			X	X
12	Puako Petroglyphs		X			.7	½		74	2	29	1	X	X	X							X
13	Kiholo Bay		X			2.0	1		87	2	17	1/2			X	X	X	X			X	
14	Kaloko-Honokohau		X			2.0	1		100	2½	4	1/4			X	X	X	X			X	X
15	Captain Cook Monument			X		2.5	2	500	113	3	14	1/2	X		X	X		X			X	X
16	City of Refuge	X				1.0	1		111	3	20	3/4			X			X			X	X
17	South Point		X			3.0	1		80	2	64	1½	X	X	X	X		X			X	X
18	Mauna Kea Summit				X	6.0	8-10	4176	35	1	62	2	X	X		X	X		X		X	

altitude. They also require good footwear and more equipment.

Obviously, hiking time varies from person to person, depending on such factors as pace and the extent to which one chooses to linger for lunch and to swim where pools exist. The time noted in the Hiking Chart is based on a leisurely pace. Trail distance is based either on an exact measurement or on an approximation with the aid of a topographic map.

Driving time and mileage cited are based on the posted speed limit and are measured both from Hilo and from Kailua-Kona. Specific driving instructions are provided preceding each hike description.

The equipment noted on the Hiking Chart is minimal for hiking. As a rule, however, I always carry water, food and a first-aid kit. Although the choice between tennis shoes and hiking boots is listed in some cases as optional, I prefer hiking boots in most cases. Obviously, your feet are an important consideration in hiking since it is common on an island that has experienced extensive volcanic activity to have volcanic ash or rock underfoot. Usually, shorts or long pants are optional, except in those cases where the brush is thick or when the weather requires warmer clothing.

Drinking water is available from streams in many areas, but it should be boiled, treated, or filtered, since cattle, pigs and goats usually share the water supply. To avoid the chance of illness, carry one quart of water per person. In many cases, firewood is at a premium. A small, light, reliable backpacking stove is a convenience and a comfort if you plan to cook out.

Before each hike description you will find the hike rating, trail features, hiking distance and time, specific driving instructions, and introductory notes. On some hikes it is necessary to walk on private property. Information and addresses are provided so that you can secure permission in advance. Permission is usually readily granted either over the telephone or in person when you sign a liability waiver.

In the trail narrative I usually mention the flora and fauna to be seen along the way, especially the unusual and the unique, in an effort to add to your hiking enjoyment. But I don't mention everything, and you may wish to buy one of several guides to plants and animals of the islands, available at many stores.

Preceding each trail narrative is a map to help you find the trailhead and to locate trail highlights. The maps show many features of the hikes as well as camping information. The maps are not to scale.

The County of Hawaii offers daily public transit service from Hilo to Kona and from Hilo to Hawaii Volcanoes National Park. When available, bus transportation to the trailhead is cited. Contact the Hawaii County Transit System for more information and schedules. Hitchhiking is presently legal, but rides are hard to get, especially in outlying areas.

SAFE HIKING

In 1989, the State Department of Health issued a warning to campers and hikers that portable water filters will not protect them from the dangerous bacterium leptospirosis. Health officials say that only boiling or chemical treatment will control this disease that is found in surface water throughout Hawaii. It enters the body through breaks in the skin or through mucous membranes and can cause flu-like symptoms. The disease can also be fatal.

Portable water filters may protect against giardia, salmonella and other bacteria and parasites, but not leptospirosis. The department's release stated that vigorous boiling is the only reliable method of purification. Tablets containing hydroperiodide will work if boiling is not possible, according to health authorities.

Hawaii is a relatively safe island to hike and camp. Nevertheless, you should take precautions as you would on the mainland. The fact is that most of the violence directed against hikers and campers is drug related. A person looking for drugs is looking for trouble. You are cautioned never to hike or camp alone. As a general rule, the farther you hike and camp away from populated areas, the safer your experience is likely to be. NEVER leave valuables unprotected. I always carry a daypack containing those items which I cannot afford to lose - wallet, airline ticket, camera - and I carry it everywhere. Yes, even there!

One problem facing the hiker on Hawaii is the lack of trailhead signs and trail markers. Most of the trails contained in this book are well-defined, but most are not posted. Although I provide detailed directions to the trailhead and a trail narrative that makes the trail easy to follow, seasonal rains, floods, and other natural forces impact on the land to alter it, sometimes significantly. Additionally, trail markers are sometimes destroyed or removed, I suspect, by locals who are either mischievous or who wish to discourage visitors to their favorite places. Good judgment and a regard for the time-tested rules of hiking are good protection.

Hikers and campers are always relieved to learn that there are no poisonous snakes nor is there any poison ivy and poison oak in Hawaii. Poisonous centipedes and scorpions are found at low elevations. The two biggest pests in Hawaii are the mosquito and the cockroach. While neither is fatal to man, both are troublesome. They can make an outdoor experience disagreeable unless precautions are taken. You will have to live with the cockroach, but all the mosquito lotions and sprays seem to provide effective protection. Due to the wet climate, be prepared to make frequent applications.

In order to ensure a safe and enjoyable experience and to protect the environment remember:
1. Do not hike alone.

2. Many Hawaiian trails are wet and slippery, and the terrain is loose and brittle. Wear sound shoes.
3. Contrary to popular belief, it is not possible to live off the land. Carry your own food.
4. Although some fruits are available, never eat or taste unknown fruits or plants.
5. Carry your own water or boil or filter water from streams.
6. A tent with a rain fly ensures comfortable and dry nights.
7. Carry your own trash out.
8. Bury personal wastes away from streams.
9. Firewood in most places is not available or is too wet for use. Carry a stove for cooking.
10. Darkness sets in right after sunset.

On the trail

Camping and Cabins

Camping out on Hawaii will add a dimension to your visit. Campgrounds on Hawaii range from adequate to good and contain most of the amenities. The price is right: all but county campgrounds are free. The camping map locates county, state, and national campgrounds as well as camping shelters and cabins.

Campgrounds in Hawaii Volcanoes National Park are on a first-come, first-served basis. There are three drive-in campgrounds in the park. The one at Namakani Paio, 3.0 miles from the visitor center, and the one at Kipuka Nene, 11.5 miles from the visitor center, have water, shelters and cooking pits. ~~The third campground, at Kamoamoa, 30 miles from the visitor center, at the southeast portion of the park, offers spacious campsites with water, tables, shelters and fireplaces but no water. In July 1989, Kamoamoa was threatened by lava from Kilauea.~~ Even in midsummer, campsites are usually available at all campgrounds. There is a seven-day limit, and campgrounds are free. I recommend Namakani Paio for a convenient and comfortable campground.

All other national park trail cabins and trail shelters are walk-in facilities. The two cabins on the trail to the summit of Mauna Loa-at Red Hill, 10,035 feet, and at the summit, 13,860 feet contain bunk beds and mattresses and, although you might

HAWAII—CAMPING

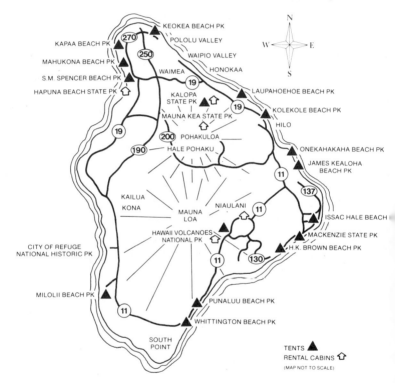

TENTS ▲
RENTAL CABINS ⌂
(MAP NOT TO SCALE)

find blankets, white gas stoves, lanterns, and some cooking utensils, you should not expect to. Carry all the necessary equipment to ensure a comfortable and safe trip (See "Food and Equipment" section). Water is available, but should be treated with purifying tablets or boiled. The trail shelters at Ka'aha, Halape, and Keauhou are simple overnight wilderness facilities with shelters, fireplaces and drinking water that should be purified or boiled. The cabin at Kipuka Pepeiao has three beds and mattresses and water that should also be treated or boiled. Check at the information desk at the Visitor Center for current water levels when you pick up your wilderness hiking permit.

Volcano House, the national park concessionaire, offers inexpensive housekeeping A-frame cabins at the Namakani Paio campground, 3 miles from the visitor center. Each cabin contains a double bed and a bunk bed accommodating a total of four persons. For $24 per night, each cabin has mattresses, linen, soap, a picnic table, outdoor barbecue grill, and a hot shower in a central washroom. Since the cabins are located at 4,000 feet, it is a good idea to bring an extra blanket or sleeping bag with you even during the summer months. Each cabin is a comfortable accommodation in a heavily wooded area. (See Appendix for address).

Permits are required when camping at McKenzie State Park on the east coast and at Kalopa State Park on the northeast side, the only state parks where camping is permitted. McKenzie is a beach park, whereas Kalopa is in a wet area and is not as conveniently located. The state parks are free, and they have water, shelter and fireplaces. Reservations are accepted and permits may be secured from the Division of State Parks.

The state also operates four comfortable and inexpensive cabin facilities on the island. They are located at Mauna Kea State Park, at Kalopa State Recreation Area, at Hapuna Beach State Recreation Area, and at Volcano (Niaulani Cabin). Mauna Kea State Park (Pohakuloa cabins) is located on the Saddle Road, 33 miles from Hilo at an elevation of 6,500 feet. Seven cabins accommodating six people each are available at $5-10 per person (the more people, the less cost per person). Each cabin contains bedding, towels, cooking and eating utensils, electricity, electric range, refrigerator, showers, and toilets. The facilities at Kalopa State Park, 42 miles from Hilo, contain the same amenities, with a central mess/recreation hall. There are two cabins with two units in each accommodating 1-8 persons in each unit. The cost ranges from $2.75–$8 per person (the more people, the less the cost per person). The six A-frame shelters at Hapuna Beach State Park, 65 miles from Hilo, are situated above Hawaii's best beach. Wow! What a spot! The wood and screened shelters are simple, containing one table, two wooden platforms for sleeping (a sleep pad or inflatable mattress is a MUST!), electricity, and a central mess hall with refrigerator and electric range that is shared with shelter users. You must bring your own cooking and eating utensils. Cold water showers and flush toilets are provided. Each shelter sleeps four and costs $7 per night. Niaulani Cabin, the fourth state cabin, is located in the community of Volcano, 29 miles from Hilo just outside Hawaii Volcanoes National Park. This single cabin accommodates six persons at a cost of $5–10 per person (the more people, the less the cost per person). It is completely furnished with a living room, two bedrooms, bedding, towels, cooking and eating utensils, electricity, hot shower, electric range and refrigerator and a one-car garage. The state and federal cabins are the best values in Hawaii and are very popular with locals and visitors. You are advised to write early for reservations. (All addresses are in the Appendix).

The County of Hawaii has established a system of beach parks which offer amenities from cold water showers and drinking water to shelters, tables and firepits (see the camping map). Camping is permitted at 13 parks. Samuel Spencer Beach Park on the west side of the island is the most popular of the county campgrounds and is frequently full during the summer months. I like Harry Brown, Mahukona, and Keokea beach campgrounds (See camping map). Permits are required in these parks and may be secured in person or by writing to the Department of Parks and Recreation. Camping is limited to one week per park during the summer months and two weeks per park at other times. Fees at county parks are $1 per day for adults and 50¢ for persons 13–17. (See Appendix for addresses).

FOOD AND EQUIPMENT

For most hikes your equipment needs are minimal. Although hiking boots are not essential on most hikes, I prefer them. I recommend strong shoes or hiking boots in the Hawaii Volcanoes National Park because of the rough lava surfaces. Drinking water is available from streams in many areas, but should be boiled because cattle, pigs and goats usually share the water supply. To avoid the chance of illness, I suggest you carry sufficient water. One quart per person to start out is recommended. In many areas, firewood is at a premium; so a small, light, reliable backpacking stove is a convenience and a comfort if you plan to cook out. Most hikers find shorts or cutoffs adequate in areas up to 8,000 feet. Even during the summer, however, warm clothing is necessary when hiking to the summit of Mauna Loa or Mauna Kea, both over 13,000 feet. Because snow and ice are not uncommon most of the year on both peaks, heavy sweaters and jackets are recommended. Hats and dark glasses are also necessary for protection from the weather and the glaring sun.

Although food is more expensive on Hawaii than on the mainland, it is readily available in the towns. You may visit a local delicatessen that prepares box lunches containing local favorites such as tempura, sweet-and-sour spare ribs and sushi. When visit a local market or roadside stand for mango, papaya, pineapple, passion fruit, and local avocado which comes in the large economy size.

The following equipment is recommended for day hikes:

Daypack
Hiking boots or tennis shoes
Plastic water bottle, quart size (one per person)
Swiss Army knife
Insect repellent
Shorts
Bathing suit
Sunscreen and tanning lotion
Sunglasses
Whistle for each child
Camera and film
Hat or sun visor
Poncho or raingear
Towel
Waterproof matches
Flashlight
"Hiking Hawaii"

Planning and preparation are particularly important for the backpacker. The following equipment is recommended for overnight hikes and for campers.

BACKPACK CHECKLIST
General Equipment
Frame and pack

Lightweight sleeping bag or blanket (heavy bag
above 4,000 feet)
Backpack tent with rain fly
Plastic ground cover
Sleep pad
Plastic water bottle, quart size
Swiss Army knife
Flashlight (it helps to explore lava tubes)
40 feet of nylon cord
First-aid kit

Cooking Gear
Backpack stove
Fuel
Cooking pots
Fork and spoon
Plastic bowl
Sierra cup
Waterproof matches

Clothing
Poncho or raingear
Pants
Shorts and/or bathing suit
Hat or bandana
Undershorts
T-shirts
Socks
Hiking boots

Toilet Articles
Soap (biodegradable)
Toothbrush/powder-paste

Part-roll toilet paper
Chapstick
Comb
Towel
Insect repellent
Sunscreen and tanning lotion
Mirror
Miscellaneous
Sun glasses
Camera and film
Plastic bags
Fishing gear
"Hiking Hawaii"

Eats along the way

HAWAIIAN MADE EASY

For your interest, throughout the text wherever a Hawaiian place name is used, I have provided a literal translation if possible. In many instances, Hawaiian names have multiple meanings and even the experts sometime disagree over the literal meaning. The meanings given here are based on the best information available and on the context in which the name is used. As students of the environment, the Hawaiians had a flair for finding the most expressive words to describe their physical surroundings.

Most visitors are reluctant to try to pronounce Hawaiian words. But with a little practice and a knowledge of some simple rules, you can develop some language skill and add to your Hawaiian experience. Linguists regard Hawaiian as one of the most fluid and melodious languages of the world. There are only twelve letters in the Hawaiian alphabet: five vowels, a, e, i, o, u, and seven consonants, h, k, l, m, n, p, w. Hawaiian is spelled phonetically. Correct pronunciation is easy if you do not try to force English pronunciation onto the Hawaiian language. Vowel sounds are simple: a=ah; e=eh; i=ee; o=oh; and u=oo. Consonant sounds are the same as in English with the exception of w. The w rule is not adhered to with any consistency by local people.

Generally, w is pronounced "w" at the beginning of a word and after a. For example, Waimea is pronounced "Wai-may-ah" and wala-wala is "wah-lah-wah-lah." Hawaiians usually pronounce w as "w" when it follows o or u: auwaha is "ah-oo-wah-hah," and hoowali is "hoh-oh-wah-lee." When w is next to the final letter of a word, it is variably pronounced "w" and "v"; Wahiawa is "wah-he-ah-wa," but Hawi is "ha-vee." Listen to the locals for their treatment of this sound. Since the Hawaiian language is not strongly accented, the visitor will probably be understood without employing any accent.

Some common Hawaiian words:

'aina	land
ali'i	royalty; chief
aloha	welcome; love; farewell
aloha nui loa	much love
hale	house
haole	foreigner; Caucasian
hapa haole	part Caucasian
heiau	pre-Christian temple
hukilau	fish pull
kahili	feather standard
kahuna	priest
kai	sea
kama'aina	native born
kane	male
kapu	keep out

kaukau	food
keiki	child
kokua	help
mahalo	thanks
makai	toward the sea
malihini	newcomer
mele	song
ohana	family
'ono	delicious
'opu	belly
pali	cliff
paniolo	cowboy
pau	finished
puku	hole
pupus	snacks
wahine	female
wikiwiki	hurry

Some common Pidgin words:

brah	brother
da kine	whatchamacallit
hana hou	encore; again
howzit?	what's happening?
pau hana	quit work
shaka!	great!
suck 'em up	drink up
talk stink	use profane words
to da max	all the way

Part II:

Hiking Trails on Hawaii

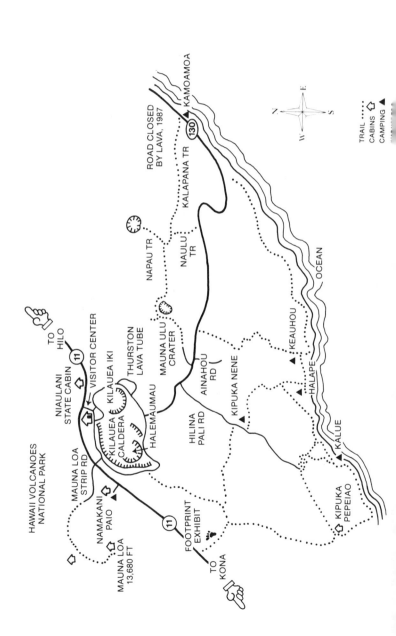

HAWAII VOLCANOES NATIONAL PARK

(Hiking Area No. 1)

Rating: See individual hikes.

Features: Most active volcano in the world, lava flows, national park from sea to summit (13,677 feet), wilderness camping, Nene (rare Hawaiian state bird), camping, 23 hiking trails.

Permission: Written permits (free) required for hiking and camping in wilderness areas may be secured at the visitor center in person or by mail (address the park superintendent). Camping is limited to 7 days per campground per year.

Hiking Distance and Time: See individual hikes.

Driving Instructions:

From Hilo (30 miles, 1 hour) south on Route 11 to Park Entrance.

From Kona (95 miles, 2 1/2 hours) south on Route 11 to Park Entrance.

Introductory Notes: Some visitors to Kilauea are amazed that they can walk to within feet of molten lava. Others are excited by being able to hike within the park from sea level to over 13,000 feet. Still others marvel at the fact that natural forces have added over hundreds of acres of land to the park since 1969. As recently as November 29, 1975, about 13 acres of land were lost as land settled into

Welcome to Hawaii Volcanoes National Park!

the sea in the Halape region of the park - the site of a wilderness camping area - as a result of a 7.2-magnitude earthquake and a tsunami (seismic sea wave). The once beautiful lagoon at Halape and hundreds of coconut trees were lost. Yet it is typical of Hawaii that simultaneously about 28 acres of land were added as a result of seaward fault movements. The result was a gain of 15 acres!

Change, change, and still more change is the attraction that draws hikers to the black-sand beaches and the lava-strewn slopes of Hawaii. It is the excitement, the anticipation that one can witness the elemental forces of nature at work close up and still survive. Of course, not everyone does survive. The toll of the November 1975 quake was one hiker killed and another still missing and presumed dead. Still more change has been taking place at the time of this writing (August, 1989). Kilauea has been erupting along its southeast rift for 68 months, emitting an average of 650,000 cubic yards of lava daily. The result to date has been the closing of the Chain of Craters Road (March 1987) when lava flowed over it in several places, the destruction of the Wahaula Visitor Center (June, 1989), the destruction of 71 homes, and the creation of a striking black sand beach at Kamoamoa. Most exciting, visitors were able to walk as close to the flowing lava as the heat allows; close enough to roast marshmallows!

Be alert!

Hawaii Volcanoes National Park, established in 1916, includes Kilauea, the most active volcano in the world, and Mauna Loa volcano. Kilauea volcano is 4,077 feet in elevation, while the summit caldera of Mauna Loa presides at 13,677. The park's total land area is 344 square miles - at least that is what it was at the time of this writing. It is no exaggeration to note that this is subject to natural change.

For convenience, I have divided the park into four hiking areas. The division is somewhat natural, for each area has some unique characteristics. First, the Mauna Loa Strip Road area has the most difficult hike on the island - the 19.6 mile hike to the summit of Mauna Loa. Second, the Kilauea caldera area is the most popular hiking area. Most of the hikes here are short and easy, and perhaps the most exciting, for two trails cross the floors of active volcanoes. Third, the Kau Desert area is a hot, arid, somewhat barren area where hiking is strenuous and yet rewarding, for most of the trails cross recent lava flows, while others lead to the coastal wilderness areas of the park. Fourth, the Kalapana area is the area where, in 1969, Madame Pele erupted along a line of fissures southeast of the Kilauea caldera and buried three miles of the Chain of Craters Road, thus isolating the Kalapana section of the park. Subsequent eruptions cut off more of the road. In June 1979 a new Chain of Craters Road was reopened, thus completing the so-called Golden Triangle, which enabled a visitor to travel from Hilo

to Hawaii Volcanoes National Park without dou-
bling back on the same highway. But then in March,
1987, successive eruptions flowed over the road,
thus closing it again, and it remains closed to date
(August, 1989) — until further notice!
Consequently, the only access to the Kalapana area
is from the Kilauea Visitor Center. Hiking trails
here take you to some of the best examples of petroglyphs on the island and to an abandoned
Hawaiian village.

In planning your hiking in the park, consult the
Hiking Chart and the maps in this guide. The former
will help you select hikes that fit your interests, time
schedule, and physical condition. The maps will re-
veal connecting trails and combinations of trails to

Hot foot — Hawaiian style!

return you to your starting point or to a convenient location for transportation.

Camping in the park is enjoyable for a couple of reasons. It's free whether you use the "civilized" campgrounds, the wilderness campgrounds or the cabins on Mauna Loa. These accommodations are also uncrowded and comfortable. Permits are necessary only to use the trail cabins and the wilderness campgrounds. See the area maps for the location of camping areas and the "Camping and Cabins" section for information about camping accommodations.

For safety, you MUST register with the park rangers at the visitor center for overnight hiking and for use of wilderness camping areas.

Namakani Paio Campground is 3.0 miles from the visitor center and Kipuka Nene Campground is 11.5 miles. Both are drive-in campgrounds and do not require permission to use. Be prepared for wet ground and rain at Namakani Paio most of the year. Shelters, fireplaces and water are available at both campgrounds. There is no drinking water at Kamoamoa Campground in the Kalapana area. Inexpensive rental cabins are also available at Namakani Paio.

Because the hiking surface ranges from hard crusted lava to soft volcanic ash and cinders, sound hiking boots are recommended for protection and comfort. A poncho is suggested in the Kilauea caldera area, which receives 95 inches of rain annually. Sun protection is a good idea in all other areas.

Mauna Loa Strip Road Area

The most notable trek in this hiking area is the climb to the summit of Mauna Loa. It is the most difficult and demanding hike on the island, due to the elevation gain. However, do not overlook the short, easy hike around Kipuka Puaulu for an informative introduction to Hawaiian flora and fauna. The two hikes in this area are off the Mauna Loa Strip Road, which begins about two miles west of the visitor center off Route 11. The strip road, though narrow, is paved and well maintained.

Kipuka Puaulu, 1.1 mile loop, 1 hour (trail rating: family).
Visitor Center to Trailhead, 4 miles by car.

The trailhead is marked by an interpretive exhibit a short distance up the Mauna Loa Strip Road. It explains that a kipuka is an area in a forest that has been ringed by successive flows of lava. These island gardens represent the interplay of geological and biological forces. Some believe that Madame Pele, the goddess of volcanoes, spares these places from lava flows so that the birds and other animals can find a sanctuary.

On the Trail: The National Park Service provides a free guide at the trailhead which is numbered to correspond to the numbered stakes along the trail. Kipuka Puaulu (probably "loop of growing flowers") is a level walk over a broad, well-defined trail. You will find a variety of flora identified and may see a number of native birds. The apapane

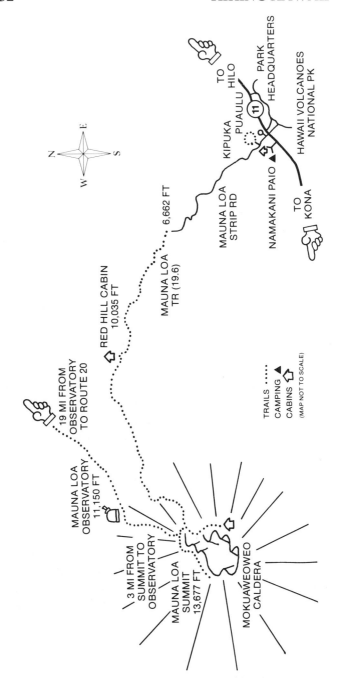

TO HILO

PARK HEADQUARTERS

HAWAII VOLCANOES NATIONAL PK

11

KIPUKA PUAULU

NAMAKANI PAIO

TO KONA

MAUNA LOA STRIP RD

6,662 FT

MAUNA LOA TR (19.6)

RED HILL CABIN 10,035 FT

19 MI FROM OBSERVATORY TO ROUTE 20

MAUNA LOA OBSERVATORY 11,150 FT

3 MI FROM SUMMIT TO OBSERVATORY

MAUNA LOA SUMMIT 13,677 FT

MOKUAWEOWEO CALDERA

TRAILS ......
CAMPING ▲
CABINS ⇩
(MAP NOT TO SCALE)

N E S W

(Himatione sanguinea) and the i'iwi (Vestiaria coccinea) are frequently confused. The apapane is a crimson bird with black wings and tail and a slightly curved black bill, while the i'iwi is a bright vermillion bird with black wings and a long, curved, salmon-colored bill. It also has orange legs, as distinguished from the apapane's black legs. Both birds are a bit over 5 inches long.

The high "tseet" of the amakihi (Loxops virens) emanates from the branches of the koa, ohia and mamane trees as this small (4 1/2") green and yellow bird forages for insects and nectar. A fine booklet published by the Hawaii Audubon Society ("Hawaii's Birds") is extremely helpful in identifying birds. It is beautifully illustrated and easy to use.

Hawaiian raspberries, or akala (Rubus hawaiiensis), are abundant along the trail and can be sweet and tasty. Look for the deep red or purplish berries.

Mauna Loa trailhead

Mauna Loa Summit, 19.6 miles, 3–4 days, 7015-feet gain (trail rating: difficult).
Visitor Center to Trailhead, 14 miles by car

Trailhead to Red Hill Cabin, 7.5 miles, 3373-feet gain on foot only
Red Hill Cabin to Summit Cabin, 11.6 miles, 3215-feet gain on foot only.
Red Hill Cabin to Summit, 12.1 miles, 3642-feet gain on foot only.

The ascent of Mauna Loa should be attempted only after considerable planning and preparation. Bear in mind that even if you take 3 or 4 days, there is a considerable altitude change and mountain sickness is a possibility. Another consideration is hypothermia, which sets in when the body is not able to generate enough heat to keep the vital organs warm. Therefore, even during the summer, carry warm clothing and a warm sleeping bag. The cabins at Red Hill and at the summit may contain blankets, white-gas stoves, lanterns, heaters and some cooking and eating utensils, but it's best to carry your own equipment. The water at each cabin, collected from roof runoff, should be boiled or treated with purifying tablets. Both cabins are free, but you must sign up with the ranger at the visitor center for their use and for hiking permits (they must know who is where in case Pele causes a disturbance).

You should allow at least two days for the ascent: one day to hike to Red Hill (7.5 miles, 3,373

Mauna Loa from Kileaua

feet gain), and another day to hike to the summit (12.1 miles, 3,642 feet gain). You will probably find that 4 days are necessary for the round trip unless you are a good hiker in good condition.

On the Trail: The trailhead (6,662 feet) is at the end of the Mauna Loa (lit., "Long Mountain") Strip Road some 14 miles from the Kilauea Visitor Center. There is a parking area and a picnic shelter at road's end. You can hitchhike to this trailhead if you don't have a car.

The excitement of this hike begins immediately. At the trailhead look for the nene (Branta sandvicensis), the Hawaiian state bird. After disappearing, this native goose was reintroduced to Maui in 1962 and has since increased in numbers. It is estimated

Nene Goose — State Bird

that about 1,000 nenes are surviving on Hawaii and Maui. The Park Service has a program to raise goslings and to return them to the wild in due course. Natural breeding is difficult owing, in part, to a number of introduced predators, such as mono-gooses, pigs, and feral dogs and cats, for whom the eggs and the young goslings are easy prey. The nene has adapted to its rugged habitat on the rough lava flows far from any standing or running water, and some people suggest that this water fowl is more ac-curately regarded as a lava fowl. The most notice-able anatomical change has been the reduction of webbing between the toes, which better suits its ter-restrial life. Its size (22-26") and its variety of muted calls, often resembling the "moo" of a cow, make it easy to identify. If you spot a nene, don't be surprised if it walks up to you. They are very friendly birds and have been known to enjoy a petting!

The trail passes through a gate in a fence designed to protect the park from feral goats, whose voracious eating habits tend to denude the vegetation. Be sure to close the gate. Soon you are above the open ohia (Metrosideros collina) forest at the 8,300-foot level. The bright red blossom of the ohia lehua, the flower of the island of Hawaii, is regarded as sacred to Pele. Legend holds that if a person picks this flower on the way to the mountain, it will rain.

The Red Hill cabin at 10,035 feet is a welcome sight in what is now open country with little growth. It is a comfortable overnight facility and offers a panorama of the island. On a clear day you can see Maui to the northwest and its summit Haleakala - the house of the sun. If you are suffering from altitude sickness - a headache and a nauseous feeling - Red Hill is a good place to lie down with your head lower than your trunk and perhaps to take an aspirin. Remember to boil or treat the water.

An early start on the second day will enable you to make a few miles before the hottest part of the day. Your hike to the summit follows the northeast rift of Mauna Loa, where you will find some startling cracks and shapes in the strata caused by recent splatter cones and lava flows. The last eruption along this rift, in 1942, extended over a 2.8-mile area. The lava flowed to within 12 miles of the city of Hilo.

About two miles from the summit, you finally arrive at the North Pit of the great Mokuaweoweo (lit., "fish section" - red part of a fish, which suggests volcanic fires) caldera. The giant Mokuaweoweo caldera is an oval depression 3 miles long, 1 1/2 miles wide, and as deep as 600 feet. The trail to the cabin drops into the caldera and crosses the smooth, flat surface, skirting to the right of Lua Poholo, a deep pit crater formed since 1841. If you haven't fallen into Lua Poholo, the cabin is a short hike up to the rim of Mokuaweoweo. You'll find water at the cabin or ice in a lava crack, a short (1/2 mile) walk southwest of the cabin. Remember to boil or treat the water.

To reach the summit you must return to the junction on the north side of the caldera and follow the ahus (rock cairns) to the 13,680-foot summit. At the summit you are standing on the top of the world's largest active shield volcano and the largest single mountain on earth, when you consider that it rises about 30,000 feet above its base on the ocean floor.

Mauna Loa has been surprisingly quiet for 40 years. The last eruption from Mokuaweoweo caldera was in 1949, when more than half the caldera floor was blanketed with new lava. The eruption of Mauna Loa in 1950, the greatest since

1859, was along the southwest rift, with fissures from, 11,000 feet down to 8,000 feet. Lava flowed westward and southeastward, and within a day had reached the sea. When lava entered the water, it boiled and steam clouds rose 10,000 feet into the air. An estimated billion tons of lava destroyed two dozen buildings and buried a mile of highway. No lives were lost.

The return trip to the trailhead is easy, but tiring if you do it in one day. An alternative return is to take the Observatory Trail. From the summit, return along the trail for 1.6 miles to a spur trail that goes northwest (left) for 0.3 mile to the emergency four-wheel-drive road and the Observatory Trail. The trail is on the left side of the road, extending for 3 steep and difficult miles to the Mauna Loa weather observatory at 11,150 feet while the road switch-backs to the observatory. Unless you have made arrangements for someone to drive to the observatory to pick you up, it is 19 miles from the observatory to Route 20, and 28 miles on Route 20 to Hilo.

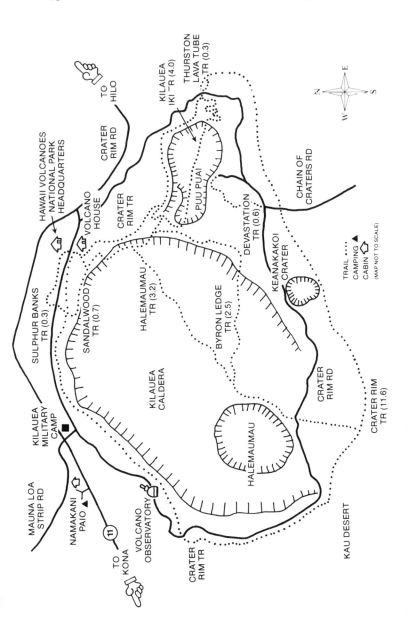

KILAUEA CALDERA AREA

Without question, the Kilauea (lit., "spewing" - referring to eruptions) section of the national park is the most exciting place on the island because dramatic change is ever imminent. Like Mauna Loa, Kilauea is a shield volcano with a characteristic broad, gently sloping dome. While the summit is 4,000 feet above sea level, the base of the mountain extends another 16,000 feet to the ocean bottom. The summit caldera, 2 1/2 miles long and 2 miles wide, contains Halemaumau, the "fire pit", which is the legendary home of Pele, the goddess of volcanoes. Halemaumau had an almost continuously active lake of liquid lava through the 19th century and the first quarter of the 20th. One commentator in 1826 noted that "the bottom was covered with lava, and the southwest and northern parts of it were one vast flood of burning matter, in a terrific state of ebullition, rolling to and fro its 'fiery surge' and flaming billows...". Today, Kilauea caldera is not as active or quite as romantic, but it continues to provide visitors with some exciting moments and thrilling experiences. Presently, (August, 1989) Kilauea has been erupting along its southeast rift about a dozen miles from the caldera on and off for 68 months. As a consequence, the Chain of Craters Road was overrun with lava and closed in March, 1987, the Wahaula Visitor Center was burned in June, 1989, and 71 homes have been destroyed over

Across Kilauea Caldera

the period. On the plus side, a marvelous black sand beach was created at Kamoamoa.

The Kilauea portion of the park is the most popular hiking area on the island because of the presence of active Kilauea and because of easy access to well-marked hiking trails. In planning your hiking, consult the maps and the text for connecting trails, since most of the trails do not loop. For example, one hike that I would recommend is to take the Halemaumau Trail across the caldera to the "fire pit", connect with the Byron Ledge Trail to the Kilauea Iki Trail, which ends at the Thurston Lava Tube, and then return to the visitor center via the Crater Rim Trail. This is approximately a 10-mile loop. No special equipment is necessary. However, I recommend a strong, durable pair of boots or shoes, water, sun protection and food.

Crater Rim Trail, 11.6 mile loop, 5-8 hours (trail rating: strenuous).
Trailhead at Volcano House.

The best introduction to the Kilauea area is to drive the Crater Rim Road or to hike the Crater Rim Trail, which encircles the caldera. It is a strenuous hike with a 500-foot elevation gain. Plan on the better part of a day to complete the hike. You will want to make some side trips to take in some of the sights and to pause frequently to enjoy the striking panoramas of the volcanic landscape.

The "fire pit" from Crater Rim Trail

On the Trail: Pick up the trail in front of the Volcano House and hike counterclockwise (right) in order to pass through the warm Kau Desert in the early morning. The trail initially passes a few steaming vents, which seem to set the mood. At "Steaming Bluff" billowing steam clouds rise from the ground, caused by water getting into the "plumbing" of Kilauea. The steam is accompanied by small amounts of hydrogen sulfide, which smells like rotten eggs. This condition is an eerie introduction to your hike.

The trail continues along the crater rim, passes the Kilauea Military Camp on the opposite side of the road, and climbs slightly up Uwekahuna (lit., "wailing priest") Bluff to the site of the Hawaii

Volcano Observatory. From here, scientists have been keeping a watchful eye on Kilauea since 1911, when Dr. Thomas A. Jagger established the observatory. Today, studies continue under the direction of the U.S. Geological Survey. Take time to visit the museum where displays explain the history, culture, and geology of the islands. It is also a good place from which to view Halemaumau and Kilauea and, on a clear day, to admire the striking presence of towering Mauna Loa to the west. This, the highest point on the trail, was once a sacred point for Hawaiians, where offerings were made to the gods.

From the observatory, the trail dips south along the road and then crosses it to the southwest rift of Kilauea and to the trailhead for the Kau Desert region. It was along the southwest rift that an eruption occurred in 1971 which lasted five days and covered an area of 1.3 square miles. A rift is a highly fractured land area on the flank of a volcano along which most of the volcano's eruptions take place.

You might choose to take the Halemaumau Trail to the "fire pit." The fire pit is about a mile off the rim trail across the Crater Rim Road to the east side of the caldera (see the Halemaumau Trail below). If not, you will at least smell the sulfur fumes being emitted by Halemaumau.

The Keanakakoi (lit., "cave of the adzes") Crater marks the beginning of the east rift zone, where in 1974 one of the last major eruptions of Kilauea occurred. During the first part of the year, the Kilauea caldera began to swell, and increased earthquake activity was recorded. Finally in July, rifts opened on the southeastern caldera rim and in the caldera floor, while 200-foot fountains of incandescent lava spurted from fissures. Lava filled Keanakakoi Crater and flowed beyond to cover the Chain of Craters Road.

From here to the fern forest you should find many ohelo (Vaccinium reticulatum) shrubs bearing delectable bright red berries. A small native shrub in the cranberry family, it has many branches with small, rounded, toothed leaves. The berries are edible but sacred to Pele. To avoid Pele's wrath, you should throw half your berries into the fire pit saying,

> E Pele, here are your ohelos.
> I offer some to you.
> Some I also eat.

After crossing the Chain of Craters Road, the trail passes through a sparsely wooded area before entering a thick tree-fern forest. Here you will find some outstanding specimens of Hawaiian tree ferns. The hapuu (Cibotium splendens) is an endemic fern that can reach 16 feet in height. In old Hawaii, hats were made from the stems. The starchy trunk core was used for cooking and as soap for washing. Another endemic tree fern is the amaumau (Sadleria splendens), from which the fire pit Halemaumau (lit., "house of ferns") derives its name. The fronds

Tree ferns

were used for thatching house frames and for making red dye to color tapa cloth.

Ample rain - about 95 inches annually - sustains this verdant and enchanting forest. The forest is shaded by a canopy of ohia lehua (Metrosideros collina) trees with red powder-puff-like blossoms which were regarded as sacred to Pele. Hawaiians believed that it would rain if the flower was picked.

The Thurston Lava Tube is a short spur trail off the Crater Rim Trail; it takes you through a 450-foot lava tunnel (see Thurston Lava Tube Trail description).

Pick up the Crater Rim Trail by crossing the road and parking lot from the lava tube. The trail follows the edge of Kilauea Iki crater (see the

Kilauea Iki Trail description). Kilauea Iki is a pit crater immediately adjacent to the eastern edge of Kilauea caldera. The trail is shaded and cool and offers a number of lookout points with interpretive exhibit cases.

The trail and the road along Waldron Ledge were closed after the November 1975 earthquake when some of the ledge fell into the crater and much of the road was severely fractured. The trail and road have since been repaired or rerouted, and it is safe to proceed and to view the power of nature first hand. A short walk will return you to Volcano House.

Halemaumau Trail, 3.2 miles, 2 hours (trail rating: hardy family).
Trailhead at Volcano House.
As you approach the trail across the lava lake floor of the Kilauea caldera, you may be apprehensive. Knowing that the earth is boiling below your every step can be overwhelming. Consequently, while the hiking is irresistible, you can't wait to finish the hike and get out of the caldera.

If your starting point is Volcano House, you might plan a loop trip (consult maps) or arrange to be picked up on the opposite side unless you plan to return across the crater.

On the Trail: The trail begins west (to the right) of the Volcano House and descends through a lush tree-fern forest, passing rocks that have fallen and rolled into the crater. The trail drops about 500 feet, intersecting the Crater Rim Trail, the Sandalwood Trail and the Byron Ledge Trail, before it crosses the floor of the caldera.

Many of the native and introduced plants are identified by marker in the forest, dominated by the ohia lehua tree with its red powder-puff-like blossoms and by Kahalii ginger with its magnificent foot-high yellow blossoms.

The hike across the floor is hot and dry, so sun protection and water are important. As you approach the rough, brittle, twisted, broken surface, an eerie, somewhat uncomfortable feeling sets in, so that as a piece of rock crumbles underfoot, you swallow hard and breathe a bit more deeply for a moment. The trail is well marked with ahus (rock cairns) and is easy to follow. The shiny black surface of the pahoehoe (smooth and ropy surface) lava sometimes nearly blinds you. The first half mile is fresh lava from a 1974 flow. In fact the trail crosses lava dating from 1885, 1954, 1971 and 1975. See if you can notice the difference.

The caldera has literally had its ups and downs over the years as it has been filled and emptied by successive eruptions. The depth of the caldera changes with almost every eruption as the floor swells and erupts. Some craters fill up and others shrink.

Beyond the junction with the Byron Ledge Trail, the Park Service has constructed a safe viewing overlook into Halemaumau, the "fire pit" and the home of the goddess Pele. Typically, there are steam clouds mixed with hydrogen sulfide, creating an unpleasant "rotten egg" odor. From here you can view the panorama from left to right, beginning with the summit of Mauna Loa, the crater rim with the Volcano Observatory, the Steaming Bluffs, Volcano House and Byron Ledge, dividing Kilauea from Kilauea Iki.

The trail continues across the Crater Rim Road to connect with the Crater Rim Trail. However, you may choose to return via the Byron Ledge Trail or the Rim Road.

Byron Ledge Trail, 2.5 miles, 1 1/2 hours (trail rating: strenuous).
Trailhead off Halemaumau Trail or Kilauea Iki Trail on foot only.

This is a convenient trail to connect with other trails or to return to park headquarters after hiking the Halemaumau Trail.

On the Trail: From the fire pit, the trail crosses Kilauea caldera eastward and climbs a few hundred feet to Byron Ledge, which separates Kilauea from Kilauea Iki. From the bluff you have views of both craters and of Puu Puai (lit., "gushing hill"), a 400-foot cone of pumice and ash on the south side of Kilauea Iki formed by an eruption in 1959. After the November 1975 earthquake, the ledge trail was closed due to slides on the west wall of Kilauea Iki. In the summer of 1976 Park Service trail crews re-routed the trail, enabling you to hike once again into

Kilauea Iki. The fencing here is a project to control wild pigs.

Kilauea Iki Trail, 4.0 miles, 2 1/2 hours (trail rating: strenuous).
Trailhead off Byron Ledge Trail on foot or from Thurston Lava Tube, 3 miles from Visitor Center by car.
    On the Trail: The Kilauea Iki (lit., "little Kilauea") Trail is accessible from Thurston Lava Tube or from Volcano House via the Halemaumau, Byron Ledge, or Crater Rim Trail. From Byron Ledge or Crater Rim, the trail descends 400 feet into the crater. This newly constructed trail was built

Kileaua Iki lava vent

after slides covered the old trail following the earthquake of November 1975. The trail bisects the crater floor, which is covered with fresh lava from a spectacular 1959 eruption. This eruption, which lasted 36 days, had exploding fountains that reached a record-setting 1,900 feet in height. Cinder, pumice and ash piled up on the crater rim over five feet thick. The devastated area (see Devastation Trail description) south of the crater was created at this time, while a pool of lava 380 feet deep remained in the crater. Since then scientists have been drilling core samples in an effort to study the cooling properties of lava. You will find a number of their drilling sites and their equipment. Obviously, these should be left undisturbed.

After the trail snakes about 400 feet up the western wall of the crater through an ohia tree-fern forest, it ends in the parking lot at Thurston Lava Tube.

Thurston Lava Tube Trail, 0.3 miles, 15 minutes (trail rating: family).
Visitor Center to Trailhead, 3 miles by car.

This is a short but a "must" trail in the Kilauea section. You can drive to the trail via the Crater Rim Road or hike the crater rim clockwise from Volcano House or from the western end of the Kilauea Iki Trail. This prehistoric lava tube was formed when the outer crust of a tongue of flowing lava cooled and solidified while the inner portion continued to flow and eventually emptied the tube, leaving a 450-foot tunnel as high as 20 feet in places.

On the Trail: The trail to the tube entrance descends through a lush tree-fern rain forest. Many of the plants are identified by marker. Native birds are commonly found here. With luck you may see the small (4 1/2") green and yellow amakihi (Loxops virents) foraging for food, or the vermillion i'iwi (Vestiaria coccinea) with black wings, a long, curved, salmon-colored bill and orange legs.

Devastation Trail, 0.6 miles, 15 minutes (trail rating: family).
Visitor Center to Trailhead, 4 miles by car.
   On the Trail: One of the most photographed and one of the most popular areas in the park, the

Devastation Trail

devastation area was created by a 1959 eruption in Kilauea Iki when 1,900-foot fountains showered the area with ash, pumice and spatter that buried an ohia forest, denuding the trees and leaving their skeletons standing in tribute to the eerie, strangely beautiful effects of Mother Nature. A boardwalk crosses the area to prevent passing feet from creating numerous trails. Today, (1989) new growth has altered the landscape so that it is no longer as "devastated" as originally.

You can drive to the trailhead via the Crater Rim Road. It is a one-mile hike past the Thurston Lava Tube.

Sandalwood Trail, 0.7 miles, 15 minutes (trail rating: family).
Trailhead at Volcano House.

On the Trail: The Sandalwood Trail is one of a number of short, easy trails from the visitor center to scenic overlooks of the Kilauea Caldera. The trail begins west (to the right) of Volcano House and gently descends for a hike along the caldera rim to the steam vents at Steaming Bluff. You pass through a rather dense ohia tree-fern forest where many of the plants are identified. A number of steam vents along the trail remind you of the presence of Pele and send off the "rotten egg" smell caused by hydrogen sulfide. You can return to park headquarters via the Crater Rim Trail or loop via the Sulfur Bank Trail.

Sulfur Bank Trail: 0.3 miles, 15 minutes (trail rating: family).
Trailhead at Visitors Center.

On the Trail: An interesting trail from the visitor center will take you to the sulfur banks, where volcanic fumaroles emit gases that deposit colorful minerals. This is an easy walk and an interesting sight, but the presence of the "rotten egg" smell means you won't linger very long.

Kau Desert Trailhead

KAU DESERT AREA

The Kau (lit., "to place") Desert is indeed just that - a hot, arid, dry, relatively barren and bleak area that composes the southern section of Hawaii Volcanoes National Park. There are no precise boundaries, but the desert region is considered to be all the land south of Kilauea caldera and between Route 11 in the west and the Chain of Craters Road in the east. All the trails here are long and hot, without any guarantee of water. It is an area that tests the hiker and his/her equipment, and perhaps appeals most to those who are seeking solitude. Compared to the other areas of the park, there are no sights to speak of - just a lot of lava, a lot of sun, a lot of stillness, and a lot of sweat!

Water is available at the trail shelters and at the Kipuka Pepeiao cabin, but check on availability at the visitor center before hiking. Remember, the most striking characteristic of the park is change. For example, new shelters constructed at Halape were destroyed a few months later by the November 1975 tsunami. Since then, a new shelter has been built and hundreds of coconut trees have been planted.

Halape Trail, 7.2 miles, 4 hours (trail rating: difficult).
Visitor Center to Trailhead, 10.5 miles by car.

On the Trail: The most popular trail in the Kau Desert is the Halape (lit., " crushed missing") Trail

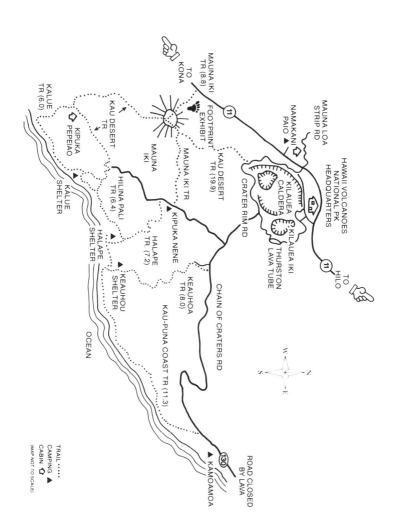

from the campground at Kipuka Nene (lit., "goose leap") to the coastal trail shelter at Halape. The well-defined trail descends through the Kau Desert about 3,000 feet to the sea. The trailhead is at Kipuka Nene Campground, a 10 1/2 mile drive over the Chain of Craters Road and the Hilina Pali Road from the visitor center. From the shelter, the trail crisscrosses a jeep road for a couple of miles and passes through low shrub and grassland. From the junction with the Hilina Pali Trail, it is less than two miles to Halape. The allure at Halape once was the oasis-like character of hundreds of coconut trees bordering a peaceful lagoon. However, on the morning of November 29, 1975, this was all changed when the island was hit by an earthquake that registered a high 7.2 on the Richter scale at the Hawaii Volcano Observatory. Roads and trails in the park were severely damaged, and at Halape a tsunami (seismic sea wave) battered the shore. This was the largest ever recorded in Hawaii, cresting at 30 feet and traveling at a staggering 187 miles per hour. Simultaneously, the land sank about six feet, an event that experts say reduced the impact of the tsunami. However, to the 32 campers at Halape, it was a nightmare, as successive waves picked up people, horses, boulders, trees and camping equipment and created a swirling mass. One camper found himself floating out to sea on the roof of the trail shelter before he jumped off and luckily swam to safety. Others were thrown into cracks in the earth, while still others clung to trees, shrubs and rocks and, thereby, to life. Miraculously, all but two campers survived. Today, calm has returned to Halape, where a new sandy beach and a cave have been formed. The Park Service worked through the summer of 1976 repairing the trail and the shelter at Halape and planting new coconut trees to replace those that were under 6 feet of water in June 1976. Some of the trunks of the coconut trees remain partly submerged in the new lagoon.

Hilina Pali Trail, 4.2 miles to Halape Junction, 4 hours (trail rating: strenuous).
Visitor Center to Trailhead, 17 miles by car.

The Hilina Pali (lit., "struck cliff") Trail begins at the end of the Hilina Pali Road From the trailhead, the Hilina Pali Trail descends the pali southeast to connect with the Halape Trail some 4.2 miles distant. In 1989, this portion of the trail was overgrown and difficult to follow. Whatever your plan, it is a hot arid hike with water available at either destination (but confirm this with a ranger first). The trail's name is derived from the Hilina Pali Fault, a dramatic example of faulting. A fault is created when a fracture occurs in the earth's crust and the block on one side moves with respect to the block on the other. During the earthquake of November 1975, the south flank of Kilauea slumped seaward along the 15-mile Hilina Pali fault to produce major effects.

On the Trail: The trail southeast from the
Hilina Pali Road descends about 2,300 feet to the
coast and to the trail shelter at Halape via the
Halape Trail or to the Ka'aha Shelter via the Kalue
Trail. The descent of the pali is a little treacherous,
but with some caution it can be negotiated safely.
After 2.2 miles the trail reaches a junction with the
Kalue Trail, which goes south 1.6 miles to the
Ka'aha Shelter on the coast. At another junction 1.2
miles beyond, the Hilina Pali Trail meets a trail that
goes southwest 1.6 miles to Ka'aha Shelter. From
this junction the trail (overgrown in 1989) goes 3.0
miles to join the Halape Trail, on which you can
head south to Halape or north to Kipuka Nene.

**Kau Desert Trail to Pepeiao Cabin, 14.4 miles, 8
hours on foot, or to Hilina Pali Overlook, 18.9
miles, 10 hours on foot (trail rating: difficult).
Visitor Center to trailhead, 3 miles by car.**

To traverse the entire length of the Kau Desert
Trail from the west side of the Kilauea Caldera to
the trail cabin at Kipuka Pepeiao requires a stout
heart, strong legs and water. This is a long, arid trail
that descends about 2,000 feet. If you have the time
(three days minimum) and are seeking solitude, a
vigorous hike can be made by taking the Kau Desert
Trail to Kipuka Pepeiao, taking the Kalue Trail to
Halape, and returning via the Halape Trail to
Kipuka Nene (32.3 miles.)

On the Trail: The trail gradually descends
through some low scrub vegetation and then across

Pahoehoe lava

relatively barren pahoehoe (smooth and ropy surface) lava. Look in the pukas (holes) for Pele's hair,
a thin, golden substance consisting of volcanic glass
spun into hairlike strands. It is plentiful on this older
lava, as is Hawaiian "snow", a whitish lichen that is
the first thing to grow on new lava. From the trail
junction with the Mauna Iki Trail, an easy, gradual
climb to the summit of Mauna Iki (3,032 feet)
provides interesting panoramas of the surrounding
area. From the summit you can take the Mauna Iki
Trail west to the "footprints" exhibit (see the Mauna
Iki Trail for their description). The rest of the trail is
an easy descent skirting the Kamakaia (lit., "the fish
eye") Hills to the cabin at Kipuka Pepeiao.

From the cabin, the trail parallels a fault system as it leads to the Hilina Pali Road and Overlook. There are a number of interesting cracks in the earth along the trail which permit you to study a fault system up close. Notice the scars and tears in the pali (cliff) walls where the earth has slipped and has been torn away. From the pali there are dramatic views of the Kau Desert and the coast.

Mauna Iki Trail, 8.8 miles, 5 hours (trail rating: difficult).
Visitor Center to Trailhead, 9 miles by car.

Crossing the Kau Desert east-west, the Mauna Iki (lit., "little mountain") Trail connects the Hilina Pali Road and Route 11 and bisects the Kau Desert Trail. This convenient trail enables the visitor to cut hiking distance and time to points of interest in the desert.

On the Trail: If you begin your hike off Route 11, you can conveniently visit the footprints exhibit. There is a highway sign noting the trailhead. From here, it is an easy 0.8 mile hike to the footprints over a broad, well-defined trail. Some of the footprints are under glass while others are in protected enclosures to prevent vandalism and to shelter them from the elements. It is here that armies assembled in 1790 to do battle for control of the island. The armies opposing Kamehameha the Great were overcome by the fumes and dust from Halemaumau, and their footprints were left in the hardening ash. Some believe that Pele interceded to assist

Kamehameha. If you search the area, you can find other footprints, although those under glass are the most distinguishable.

The trail continues to the top of Mauna Iki (3,032 feet) and to a junction with the Kau Desert Trail. The trail is well-defined by rock cairns. Some of the lava is from the recent flows of 1971. Indeed, Mauna Iki is geologically an infant, having been formed in 1920. It is a satellite shield volcano, built by lava flows from Halemaumau. There are countless cracks in the area that are part of the southwest rift of Kilauea. It is a fascinating place to investigate, but do so with caution.

From Mauna Iki follow the Kau Desert Trail north 0.7 mile to the Mauna Iki Trail, which traverses the desert to the Hilina Pali Road. Along this trail you can find handfuls of Pele's hair: thin, golden, spun volcanic glass in hairlike strands. It is also a good chance to examine and to photograph outstanding examples of pahoehoe feet and toes where the lava has naturally flowed to form footlike shapes. Additionally, you will find lava rivers, numerous pit craters and small cinder cones.

As you approach a low scrub area, the trail is not distinguishable, but if you continue due east you can't miss the road and trail's end. From here, it is about 1 mile to the campground at Kipuka Nene, 4 miles to the Chain of Craters Road and 10 1/2 miles to the visitor center.

Keauhou Trail, 8 miles, 8 hours (trail rating: difficult).
Visitor Center to Trailhead, 12 miles by car.

This trail is infrequently traveled, which may be a good reason to take it to Keauhou (lit., "new current") and to the coast. Drive the Chain of Craters road past the left turn to Mauna Ulu to a broad expanse of lava from the Mauna Ulu flow and to a turnout on the right and to the trailhead, a solitary marker in the middle of the lava field about 25 yards from the turnout.

On the Trail: The trail drops 2,500 feet to the coast. It is necessary to negotiate the Poliokeawe (lit., "bosom of Keawe") Pali. The trail is overgrown beyond the trailhead until you reach the pali. The trail is due south so you should be able to follow it.

Don't forget your wilderness permit to hike and to use the trail shelter. The ranger can also tell you about available water. Even then, the water should be treated with purifying tablets or boiled.

From Keauhou you can take the Kau-Puna Trail west to Halape or east to the Chain of Craters Road (Route 13).

...and still more lava!

Kau-Puna Trail, 11.3 miles, 6 hours (trail rating: difficult).
Visitor Center to Trailhead, 24 miles by car.

Before the Chain of Craters Road was built, the only direct connection between Kalapana and the Kilauea portion of the national park was by this foot trail. If you are looking for a long, hard, lonely hike without any available water for almost 20 miles, the Kau-Puna Trail will satisfy you. It follows the coastline from Halape to the end of the Chain of Craters Road (Route 13). It can be a very hot hike, although ocean breezes offer some relief.

On the Trail: The trail from Halape to Keauhou is a well-defined, short 1.7 miles. Check with the ranger regarding available water at Keauahou.

Initially, the trail crosses relatively old lava formations that have been eroded by the sea. There are numerous coves and sea arches where the crashing surf has performed its artistry. There are also a number of blowholes and caves where the rushing water is forced through small openings to form brilliant fountains and sprays of water.

About five miles from Keauhou, you begin to cross recent flows from Mauna Ulu. Consequently, the trail is somewhat obscure, but you can find your way by following the coast. In 1971 lava flowed over Poliokeawe and Holei palis in a spectacular display and eventually reached the sea in an even more magnificent display as the molten lava flowed into the cold ocean water. In March 1971 lava completely buried the old Hawaiian village site of Kealakomo (lit., "the entrance path") on the southern coast. This was the flow that also covered much of the Chain of Craters Road and resulted in its closure until 1979, when it was reopened and then in 1987 closed again.

As you approach the road, be on the lookout for some ancient petroglyphs. There is a small sign marking the site from the trail's end at the road.

KALAPANA AREA

The forces of nature isolated the southern section of the Hawaii Volcanoes National Park between 1969 and 1979. Beginning in 1969, a series of eruptions from Kilauea covered miles of the road connecting the Kilauea Visitor Center with the Kalapana area. For 10 years it was a 55-mile drive from the Kilauea Visitor Center to the Wahaula Visitor Center on Route 13. In 1979 the Chain of Craters road was rebuilt and reopened, enabling visitors to drive from the center of the park to the southern section. It was a scenic and pleasant ride of 32 miles from the Kilauea Visitor Center to the

Kilauea Visitor Center

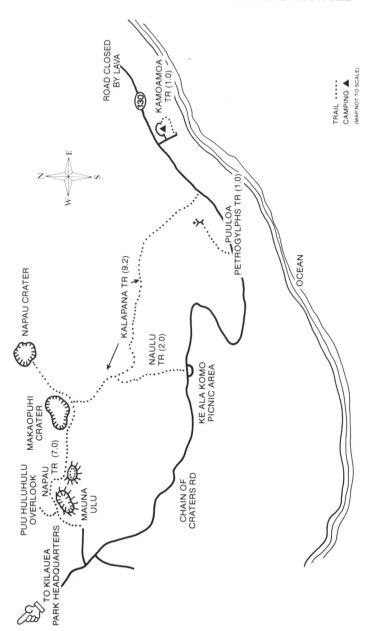

ROAD CLOSED BY LAVA

130

KAMOAMOA TR (1.0)

N
W — E
S

PUULOA PETROGYLPHS TR (1.0)

KALAPANA TR (9.2)

OCEAN

NAPAU CRATER

NAULU TR (2.0)

MAKAOPUHI CRATER

KE ALA KOMO PICNIC AREA

PUU HULUHULU OVERLOOK

NAPAU TR (7.0)

MAUNA ULU

CHAIN OF CRATERS RD

TO KILAUEA PARK HEADQUARTERS

TRAIL ·····
CAMPING ▲
(MAP NOT TO SCALE)

Wahaula visitor area. But then in 1983, Kilauea erupted along its southeast rift causing considerable damage to property and, in 1987, it overran the Chain of Craters Road thus closing it once again. Since 1983, lava has destroyed the Wahaula Visitor Center in Kalapana and 71 homes. It was still erupting in August, 1989. Most of the hiking trails in the Kalapana area are short and relatively easy.

Kamoamoa Trail, 1 mile loop, 1 hour (trail rating: family).
Visitor Center to Trailhead, 30 miles by car.
Kamoamoa is a quiet, shady campground awaiting the camper looking for solitude. Kamoamoa is the site of an ancient Hawaiian village and a black sand beach created by recent lava flows.

On the Trail: You begin the trail loop at the campground or at the parking lot. Like all Hawaiian shoreline villages, Kamoamoa was built on a bluff overlooking the sea with a generous supply of beach stones to construct dwellings and with a convenient place to launch canoes. Just past the burial grounds, the long, narrow canoe sheds are apparent. Walk directly to the beach where you can imagine ancient Hawaiians preparing to launch their outriggers. They had to drag their boats to the beach and then time their move so that the waves would pull the boat and the men out to the open sea.

A sea arch along the coast is what remains of a lava tube that has been eroded by the pounding surf. The many lava tubes found on the islands are unique

features of volcanic activity. A lava tube is formed
when the surface of a lava flow solidifies but the
molten lava within continues to flow downslope,
evacuating the surrounding crust to leave a tube.
Little remains of the dwellings at Kamoamoa because the sides and the roofs were made of wood
and grass. The floors and about three feet of the side
walls were a mixture of beach stones and lava rocks.
The rest of the walls and the roofs were constructed
of ohia poles lashed together with hau bark; pili
grass was used for thatching. The family mingled

Kamoamoa Beach

and slept in the hale noa (sleeping house), but used other houses for eating and working.

The remains of salt trays can be found near the shoreline. Salt water was poured into these stone pans and allowed to evaporate. As the crystals formed, they were moved to shallower stone pans to dry further, and then put in pans lined with ti leaves to be stored for later use. Nearby is a weather-worn papamu stone, used in a Hawaiian checker game that was extremely popular in every village. The trail passes through the campground and returns to the parking lot. CAUTION: This is an unsafe swimming beach because of strong ocean currents and riptides.

Puu Loa Petroglyphs, 1.0 mile, 3/4 hour (trail rating: hardy family).
Visitor Center to Trailhead, 26 miles.

On the Trail: The trailhead is marked by a road sign 26 miles east of the Kilauea Visitor Center. The trail to the Puu Loa (lit., "long-hill") Petroglyphs is marked and well-worn as it crosses pahoehoe lava, which has a smooth and ropy surface, unlike aa lava, which has a rough, clinkery surface. The view upcountry from the trail offers a panorama of the Kilauea eruptions of 1969 through 1972, which flowed to the sea and covered much of the Chain of Craters Road.

You will find the petroglyphs on mounds. There are hundreds, in varying sizes and shapes. There are dots, dashes, lines and bars as well as some figures

that are somewhat indistinguishable. Holes in the
ava (pukas) were receptacles in which ancient
Hawaiians placed the umbilical cords of their children to insure a long life.

**Kalapana Trail, 9.2 miles, 5 hours (trail rating:
strenuous).**
Visitor Center to Trailhead, 28 miles by car.
There is little noteworthy about the Kalapana
(lit., "announce noted place") Trail. In 1989, the
trail was overgrown and difficult to follow in places.
This trail needs to be cleared and marked. I do not
recommend it.
On the Trail: The trail begins its gradual 2,500-
foot ascent on the north side of the Chain of Craters
Road. The first half of the trail crosses mostly cen-
turies-old lava. Vegetation, a variety of ferns and
low scrub, obscure the trail. Although this is a hot,
arid area, the cool trade winds offer some relief. The
panoramas of the island are striking. The eye easily
sweeps along the coastline where numerous groves
of coconut and palm trees indicate the presence of a
trailside camping area or an abandoned fishing village. To the north and west, there is a seemingly
endless stretch of lava.
After 7 miles, patches of road between lava
flows are reminders of the power of Madame Pele,
the goddess of volcanoes. These remnants of pave-
ment are what remains of the Chain of Craters
Road, which was closed by successive lava flows in
1969. The new road has been rerouted to the

southwest in 1979 and reopened in that year only to be closed again in 1987, when lava from Kilauea overran the road. The 8-mile mark is reached at a junction with the Naulu Trail. From here, it is 1.2 miles to the Napau Trail, which in turn leads the hiker to the Kilauea area.

Naulu Trail, 2 miles, 1 hour (trail rating: hardy family).
Visitor Center to Trailhead, 14 miles by car.

The Naulu (lit., "the groves") trailhead is located on the north side of the Chain of Craters Road 14 miles from the Kilauea Visitor Center. Until the lava flows of 1972 Naulu was a popular forest and picnic area. Today, the trail is useful because it provides convenient access to the Kalapana Trail, which in turn provides access to a number of interesting craters.

On the Trail: The trail begins opposite a turnout along the Chain of Craters Road, Ke Ala Komo (lit., "entrance path"), where there was once a populous village. The first 0.2 mile of the trail, over rough aa lava, parallels the road until it emerges on a 1971 pahoehoe lava flow from Mauna Ulu. Since Naulu is a newly established trail, the lava is not worn, so it is necessary to follow the ahus, or stone piles, as you make your way north. There is no shelter or shade from the hot sun, nor any water. On the right and front right, numerous trees and a variety of scrub have survived successive lava flows. After the first mile the summit of Mauna Ulu comes into view on the front left. Near the end of the trail you reach the remains of the old Chain of Craters Road. Follow the road northwest (left) for a short distance to a junction with the Kalapana Trail. From here you have the option to take the Kalapana Trail east 8 miles to the coastline or northwest 1.2 miles to join to Napau Trail.

Napau Trail, 7 miles, 4 hours (trail rating: strenuous).
Visitor Center to Trailhead, 9 miles by car.
The Napau (lit., "the endings") area provides an opportunity to observe recent lava flows, volcanic craters, and the growth of a shield volcano. To reach the trailhead, drive on the Chain of Craters Road toward the coast and make a left turn at a sign, "Mauna Ulu." Drive a short distance to the end of the road and a trailhead marker.

On the Trial: The first part of the trail traverses the gently sloping flanks of Puu Huluhulu (lit., "shaggy hill"), a prehistoric cinder and spatter cone which stands northwest of a newly built shield volcano, Mauna Ulu (lit., "growing mountain"). Major eruptions broke out along the east rift of Kilauea in 1969, with fountains spewing forth along a fissure that paralleled the Chain of Craters Road. By June 1969 repeated flows and the accumulation of spatter and cinder had built a gently sloping, shield-shaped cone more than a mile across and 400 feet high. Thus was Mauna Ulu born. Subsequent flows filled some nearby craters and covered parts of the road.

Hot stuff!

At a junction one mile from the trailhead, a short trail on the left (north) leads to the Puu Huluhulu overlook.

Some startling shapes formed by the pahoehoe (smooth and ropy surface) lava are found along the entire length of the trail. Search the pukas (holes) in the lava for "Pele's hair," a golden, hairlike substance consisting of volcanic glass spun in gossamer form.

Beyond Mauna Ulu the trail passes north of Alae (lit., "mudhen"), a pit crater created in 1969. In that year, successive eruptions and lava flows from both Alae and Mauna Ulu alternately filled and emptied Alae Crater. It's an exciting and interesting spot.

From near Alae the trail gently descends about 3 miles to a junction with the Kalapana Trail near Makaopuhi (lit., "eye of eel") Crater, which is a crater second in size only to Kilauea. Recent eruptions (1965, 1969) from fissures on the flanks of Makaopuhi (part of the east rift zone of Kilauea) have created havoc and change; the most notable was the destruction of the Chain of Craters Road. From the Napau/Makaopuhi junction, it is two miles to Napau Crater. Not unlike its neighbors, Napau has been active in recent years. Its most dramatic contribution came in 1965 when lava from the crater created a forest of tree molds. This is another interesting place to examine, but after a long, warm hike you may not choose to linger.

Namakani Paio Campground

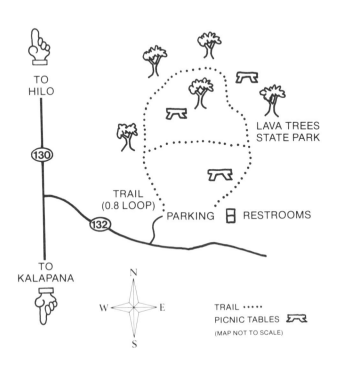

TO
HILO

130

TRAIL
(0.8 LOOP)

132

PARKING 🚻 RESTROOMS

TO
KALAPANA

LAVA TREES
STATE PARK

N

W ←＋→ E

S

TRAIL ·····
PICNIC TABLES
(MAP NOT TO SCALE)

LAVA TREES

(Hiking Area No. 2)

Rating: Family.
Features: Lava trees, native and introduced plants,
picnic.
Permission: None.
Hiking Distance & Time: 0.8 miles loop, 1/2 hour.

Driving Instructions:

From Hilo (24 miles, 3/4 hour) south on Route 11, left on Route 130, left on Route 132 to park entrance.

From Kona (130 miles, 3 1/2 hours) south on Route 11, right on Route 130, left on Route 132 to park entrance.

Introductory Notes: In 1790, Kilauea let loose her fury and spewed out more than 37 million cubic yards of lava, some of which roared through the present site of Lava Trees State Park, where ohia lehua (Metrosideros collina) trees were abundant. (Legend holds that the lehua, with its bright red stamens of 1/2 to 1 inch, are a favorite of Pele, the Goddess of Volcanoes. It is further believed that when angry, Pele will destroy groves of lehua with streams of lava.) As the lava cooled, tree-shaped shells were formed leaving some unique and exotic volcanic formations popularly called lava trees. Since then, the lehua have made a comeback and dominate the park today. WARNING: Lots of mosquitos here, so protect yourself.

On the Trail: Lava Trees is a delightful and educational short walk for the whole family. Begin your hike on the trail nearest the restrooms.

Heliconia (Heliconia humilis) is particularly abundant near the parking lot. This so-called "lobster claw" variety, commonly used in flower arranging, is identified by its bright red bracts, which resemble the claw of a boiled lobster.

Lava Tree

The largest and best examples of the lava trees are in the center of the loop trail where a connecting trail intersects. Examine these strange and bizarre formations, but avoid the temptation to pick a piece from the trees, as some thoughtless visitors have done.

At the far end of the loop, where it curves to return, look for the delicate lavender wild, or Philippine, orchid (Spathoglottis plicata). It appears to have five starlike petals, which are actually two petals and three sepals. These orchids are very common on the island and quite popular in home gardens.

When you select any of three picnic shelters or spread a blanket on the grass for lunch or a nap, you are surrounded by a veritable garden of tropical plants. In addition to those mentioned, bracken fern, torch ginger, crotons and tree ferns are identifiable.

At trail's end, warning signs caution the hikers about cracks or fissures, a further reminder of Pele's wrath. A giant kiawe (Prosopis pallida) tree reaches for the sky in spite of damage to the root system. This interesting tree with lovely, fernlike leaves, thorny branches and gnarled trunk is a valuable asset: it is a source not only of fuel and lumber but also of honey, medicine, tannin and fodder, which is produced from its beanlike yellow pods, which contain 25% grape sugar.

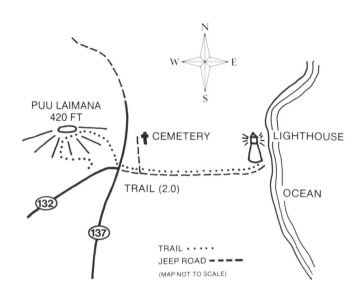

PUNA ERUPTION - 1960

(Hiking Area No. 3)

Rating: Hardy Family.
Features: Site of 1960 eruption that destroyed Kapoho Village and added 500 acres to the state.
Permission: None.
Hiking Distance and Time: 2 miles, 1 hour.
Driving Instructions:
From Hilo (28 miles, 1 hour) south on Route 11, left on Route 130, left on Route 132 to site.

From Kona (134 miles, 3 1/2 hours) south on Route 11, right on Route 130, left on Route 132 to site.

Introductory Notes: Change is very evident at Kapoho (lit., "the depression") for not only was a small but thriving village destroyed but also 500 new acres were added to the State of Hawaii as a result of the 1960 Puna eruption.

At the beginning of November 1959 as many as 1,500 earthquakes per day were being recorded at Kilauea Caldera. Then on November 14, a crack opened on the southwest wall of Kilauea Iki adjacent to Kilauea Caldera. In the succeeding days, Hawaii experienced spectacular eruptions. As a result of an unusual abundance of gas in relation to the amount of liquid lava, numerous fountains spurted forth in varying heights from 50 to 100 feet. Eventually one fountain reached an incredible 1,900 feet - the highest ever recorded.

Quiet returned for a few weeks until January 13, 1960, when an eruption broke out again on the east rift of Kilauea, 28 miles from the caldera and 1/4 mile north of Kapoho village. In the next month lava poured toward the sea and fountains of lava reached 1,500 feet in height. Finally, on February 19, it was over. The toll stood at one village destroyed, 70 buildings overcome and much valuable agricultural land lost. However, 500 acres had been added to the island.

On the Trail: An interesting hike on the crust and ash of a relatively new flow begins along the road at the site of Kapoho village at the base of Puu Laimanu (lit., "Lyman's hill"). Note the presence of "Hawaiian snow," a white lichen which is the first growth to occur on a lava flow. There are also some ferns and low scrub struggling to survive. Your walk to the rim of this cinder cone will be a slippery one indeed, but with a little care, easily achieved.

As you proceed toward the ocean following the trail of the lava flow, Pele's power and force are evident. Cross the junction of Route 132 and 137 and swing left a short distance (0.2 mile) to a small cemetery miraculously spared by the charging lava. In some instances, the flowing lava brushed past tombstones while in other places gravesites were surrounded by the lava. It's an unusual site. The hike to the sea follows a jeep road bordered by rough, clinkery aa lava. The automated lighthouse at trail's end stands on the state's easternmost point. You're as close to California as you can get in Hawaii.

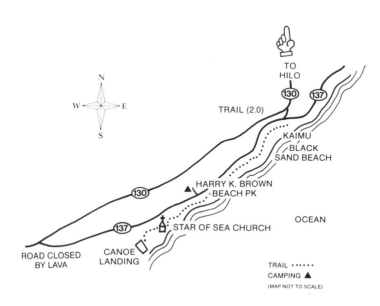

KALAPANA COASTLINE

(Hiking Area No. 4)

Rating: Hardy Family.
Features: Black sand beach, Star of the Sea Church, ancient canoe landing, camping, picnicking, swimming, surfing.
Permission: None. Camping permit for Harry K. Brown Beach Park from Dept. of Parks and Recreation in Hilo or Hale Halawai in Kona (see Appendix).

Hiking Distance and Time: 2 miles, 1 hour.
Driving Instructions:
From Hilo (32 miles, 1 hour) south on Route 11, left
on Route 130 to junction with Route 137, left on
137 to Kaimu Black Sand Beach.
From Kona (138 miles, 3 1/2 hours) south on Route
11, right on Route 130 to junction with Route
137; left on 137 to Kaimu Black Sand Beach.

Introductory Notes: "Don't go on that beach,
Charlie," cautioned a young mother. "You'll get

Kaimu Black Sand Beach

dirty." Curiously, this incorrect statement is frequently overheard on Hawaii's black sand beaches. Black sand beaches, of course, are formed by lava which reaches the sea, explodes when it hits the cold water, and then, in time, is reduced to sand by the crashing surf.

Hiking and camping along the Kalapana (lit., "announce noted place") Coast are enjoyable experiences for the young and for ocean loving people. Since the Chain of Craters Road, a few miles beyond, was closed in 1987 by a volcanic eruption, the number of visitors to the Kalapana area has decreased markedly because access to Hawaii Volcanoes National Park is no longer possible from here.

On the Trail: Park your car in the shade at Kaimu (lit., "gathering sea") Beach, a popular surfing spot on Hawaii. However, caution should be exercised, for the surf and undertow are powerful and should be challenged only by the strongest swimmers. Walking among the palms and along the coarse-sand black beach is an enchanting experience. Kaimu is probably the most photographed beach on the island.

Follow the coastline where you will be equally enchanted by the dancing surf as it charges and crashes against the rugged, jagged lava coast. The hala, or screwpine (Pandanus odoratissimus), is a common tree found on all coastal areas of the Hawaiian Islands. It is frequently referred to as "tourist pineapple," since the fruit somewhat resembles the pineapple and is jokingly identified as such to tourists by locals. The fruit is sometimes cut into sections, which are then strung to make a fruit lei. The long fibrous leaves (lauhalas) are still woven into many products by Hawaiians. They make durable floor mats, purses, hats and fans.

The beach at Harry K. Brown Park is also dangerous for swimming and should be approached with caution. Brown Park is a popular camping area and picnicking spot built on the site of the remains of Kekaloa Heiau (a pre-Christian place of worship). Look for some interesting picnic furniture made from boulders placed here by early Hawaiians.

The Star of the Sea Church, completed in 1929, is a short distance from the park. The walls and ceiling contain numerous interesting paintings, largely the work of Father Evarist Gielen, a Belgian. The small bay behind the church is the site of a stone-age canoe ramp. An interpretive exhibit explains the use of the stone slabs and tree trunks to launch outriggers. The trick in launching a canoe was to catch the receding surf at the exact moment so that the boat would be pulled out to sea before the next wave broke on it.

Pick up some groceries or food from the snack bar at the store across from the church and return to H.K. Brown Park for a swim, lunch and nap.

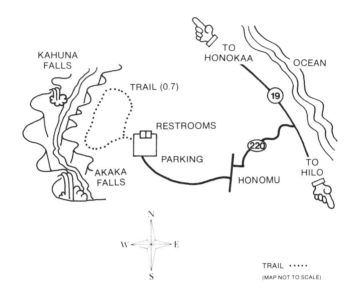

AKAKA FALLS

(Hiking Area No. 5)

Rating: Family.
Features: 420-foot Akaka Falls, Kahuna Falls, native and introduced flora.
Permission: None.
Hiking Distance and Time: 0.7 mile loop, 1/2 hour.
Driving Instructions:
From Hilo (15 miles, 3/4 hour) north on Route 19, left on Route 220 to end.

Flowers of Hawaii

Top: Kahili ginger (L), Heliconia (R)
Bottom: Plumeria (L), Shell ginger (R)

From Kona (87 miles, 2 1/2 hours) north on Route
190, right on Route 19, right on Route 220 to
end.

Introductory Notes: Few dispute that Akaka
(lit., "clearness") Falls State Park is everyone's idea
of what Hawaii is all about. It is a 66-acre tropical
paradise in a canyon park where all of nature's
riches seem larger than life. Everything - the ti, the
ginger, the bamboo, the tree ferns, the orchids, the
azaleas - comes in the large economy size!

On the Trail: A paved trail descends abruptly
from the parking lot and thrusts the hiker immediately into the canyon, where a large variety of tropical plants greets one. A guide to Hawaiian flora
such as the one by Dorothy and Bob Hargreaves
("Hawaiian Blossoms") is a handy volume to help
you identify the many varieties of plants.

Giant bamboo dominates the first part of the
trail. Bamboo has long been an important product
on the islands, having been used for fuel, furniture,
buildings, musical instruments, utensils and paper.
Indeed, bamboo sprouts are commonly eaten as a
vegetable on the islands.

Your nose will identify the delicately fragrant
yellow ginger (Zingiber zerumbet) before you see it.
It has a light-yellow blossom with olive-colored
bracts that rise at the end of a narrow tube. The
leaves are a luxuriant green. You will also find giant
torch ginger, red ginger, and shell ginger, with its
shell-like flowers. The blossom of the torch ginger

(Phaeomeria magnifica) is made up of many bracts shaped like a torch which spring up between 15-foot bamboo-like stalks with large, bright-green leaf blades. Ti (Cordyline terminalis), which is also quite abundant here, is often seen gracing the hips of hula dancers. Although some girls have switched to a plastic material, purists continue to slit ti leaves and fashion them into a skirt. This green leaf plant grows straight and tall (5-8 feet) with very shiny, thick and strong 2-3 foot blades. And there's more: banana, plumeria, ohia lehua, a variety of hibiscus (the Hawaii state flower), bird of paradise, gardenia, heliconia and azalea, to cite a partial list.

At about midpoint on the trail an overlook offers a spectacular view of Kahuna (lit., "the hidden one") Falls on the north side of the canyon. Farther up the canyon, however, is the showpiece of the park. Towering, 420-foot Akaka Falls slips over the ridge and falls lazily into Kolekole (lit., "raw, scarred") Stream, where it nourishes nature's lush gardens. Seeing it is a breathless moment in an exciting forest.

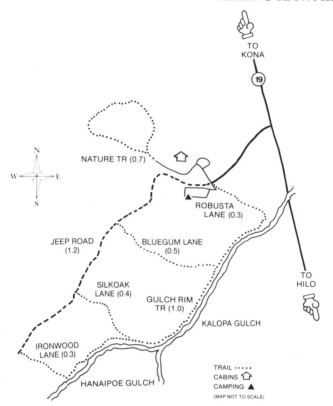

KALOPA STATE PARK

(Hiking Area No. 6)

Rating: Family.

Features: Native and introduced flora and fauna, camping, rental cabins.

Permission: None. (Camping and rental cabins from Division of State Parks - See Appendix).

Hiking Distance and Time: See individual hikes.

Driving Instructions:

From Hilo (42 miles, 1 hour) north on Route 19, left
   past 39 mile marker at sign "Kalopa State Park".
From Kona (61 miles, 1 1/2 hours) north on Route
   19, right at sign "Kalopa State Park".

Introductory Notes: Kalopa (lit., "the tenant
farmer") State Park offers the visitor not only several enjoyable hiking trails, but also comfortable,
inexpensive accommodations. You have a choice of
camping (free) or rental cabins (see "Camping" and
"Appendix" sections for details). In addition, trail
guides are available at the trailheads that detail the
flora and fauna. The only shortcoming is the 90
inches of annual rainfall making Kalopa a wet place
year round. The state park contains 100 acres of native Hawaiian rain forest and 515 acres of introduced timber species. About 95% of the 2500 native
Hawaiian plants are endemic (found no place else in
the world).

**Nature Trail, 0.7 mile, 1 hour (trail rating: fam-
ily).**
   The trail guide available at the trailhead provides information and facts about 24 posted stations
along the trail. You'll hear and see several native
and introduced birds in the forest. If you walk
slowly and speak in a low voice, you're more likely
to hear them and see them close-up. I recommend
"Hawaii's Birds," published by the Audubon

Society, as a companion guide to the park service pamphlet.

Any hike through a true Hawaiian rain forest is a delight. You will find a flat, clear, well-defined trail that is suited for persons of all ages. Many native trees flourish in the forest, but the ohia and kopiko dominate. Ohia (Metrodideros collina) — post #15 — can grow to 80 feet and, when in bloom, its lovely red, pompom-like flowers attract native birds, bees and butterflies. The flowers are a favorite of Madame Pele — the goddess of volcanoes — and it is believed that if they are picked on the way to the mountains she will envelop the visitor in a cloud of mist. However, acording to the legend, the flowers may be picked on the way out of the forest without danger. Kopiko (Psychotria hawaiiensis) — also found at post #15 — forms a tall shrub or small tree and bears shiny oblong leaves with white flowers and tiny orange fruit. The kolea (Myrsine lessertiana) is my favorite tree in the forest. It's a native whose bright pink leaves in young stages gets your attention.

On my last visit here (1989) I saw numerous kalij (Lophura leucomelana), pheasants, hens and chicks, that were introduced to Hawaii from Nepal as a game bird, although, they are protected in the park. It is a brown to black bird that has flourished here. You should also see the native elepaio (Chasiempis sandwichensis), a tiny (5 1/2 inches) bird with a loud whistle and chirping voice and a

Kalopa State Park Cabins

tail in right angle to its body. The body is white and brown with a white rump and dark tail. With luck, you may see the io, or Hawaiian hawk, the only large native bird in the forest. This endangered bird - only a few hundred in the world -with a dark body and streaked underparts, has been sighted in the forest.

Kalopa Gulch - Rim Loop, 2.8 miles, 2 hours (trail rating: hardy family).

Before hiking, be certain to secure a trail guide found at a display in the parking lot near the cabins. This hike is an easy, delightful, loop walk for the whole family. Its length can be shortened by following one of the tie trails — Bluegum Lane or Silkoak

Lane — (see map). In 1989, the trail was clear, taped and posted.

You can begin your hike from several places, but I prefer starting where Robusta Lane joins the park road near the entrance, because the trail makes a gradual ascent along the gulch and then descends the jeep road at the end of the trek. The trail initially passes through stately groves of eucalyptus and later through silk oak, paperbark, ironwood, and tropical ash. Most of the these trees were planted by the Civilian Conservation Corps for erosion control in the 1930's.

Turn right (south) when Robusta Lane meets the Gulch Rim Trail, which follows Kalopa Gulch for one mile. A short distance from the junction you will cross a small gulch and then meet the junction with Bluegum Lane. Look for guava and thimble-berries along the trail; they make a tasty snack. Guava (Psidium guajava) is a yellow, lemon-sized fruit that contains five times the amount of vitamin C than an orange. Thimbleberries (Rubus rosae-folius) are red and grow on a low bush with white flowers.

There are a few clearings which provide views into Kalopa Gulch from the trail, but the heavy growth prohibits a clear view. Before reaching Silkoak Lane, Kalopa Gulch swings left and the trail turns right and follows Hanaipoe Gulch until it meets Ironwood Lane just inside the park. The latter trail parallels pasture land until it joins the jeep road, which leads to the campground and the trailhead completing the hiking loop. Be careful walking the jeep road which is very slippery when wet.

Kalopa State Park

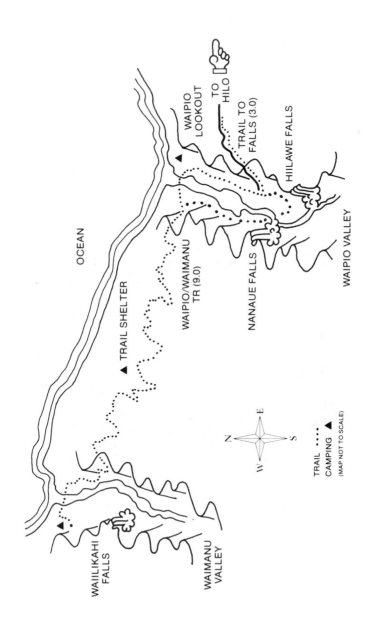

OCEAN

WAIPIO
LOOKOUT

TO
HILO

TRAIL TO
FALLS (3.0)

HIILAWE FALLS

WAIPIO/WAIMANU
TR (9.0)

▲ TRAIL SHELTER

NANAUE FALLS

WAIPIO VALLEY

WAIILIKAHI
FALLS

WAIMANU
VALLEY

N
W   E
S

TRAIL • • • •
CAMPING ▲
(MAP NOT TO SCALE)

WAIPIO/WAIMANU VALLEYS

(Hiking Area No. 7)

Rating: See individual hikes.
Features: Ancient Hawaiian settlement, native and introduced flora and fauna, wilderness camping, mountain apple, rose apple, swimming.
Permission: Call Davies Hamakua Sugar Co. (Mrs. Lorch) for camping permit in Waipio Valley.
Hiking Distance and Time: 9 miles, 7 hours.
Driving Instructions:
From Hilo (50 miles, 1 1/2 hours) north on Route 19, right on Route 240, to end of road at Waipio Lookout.
From Kona (65 miles, 2 hours) north on Route 190, right on Route 19, left on Route 240 to end of road at Waipio Lookout.

Introductory Notes: When outdoorsmen talk about hiking in Hawaii, they talk about the Kalalau Trail on Kauai, Kipahulu Valley on Maui, and Waipio and Waimanu on Hawaii. These are the ultimate in wilderness experiences in Hawaii.

Historically, Waipio and Waimanu Valleys were important centers of Hawaiian civilization, particularly Waipio (lit., " curved water"), the larger of the two. Fertile soil and ample water reportedly sustained as many as 50,000 people before the white man arrived. In the past, sugar cane, taro and bananas carpeted this six-mile valley.

In 1823 the first white men visited Waipio and found a thriving community. They were told that Waipio was once a favorite place of Hawaiian royalty; indeed, in 1780, Kamehameha is reported to have received there his war god, who singled him out as the future ruler of the islands. Later, Chinese immigrants came to Waipio, where they cultivated rice until the 1930s.

Today Waipio's population has declined to a few dozen, but taro continues to be an important crop. Most of the farmers now live in towns on the plateau east of the valley where electricity and other amenities are more readily available. Periodic tsunamis - tidal waves - have also discouraged permanent settlement. However, some people are returning to their ancestral homes upon retirement.

Guided tours of the valley are available in four-wheel drive vehicles. (It is impossible for a conventional car to negotiate the 26%-grade jeep road into the valley.) Arrangements can be made at the lookout when you arrive.

Waimanu (lit., "bird water") Valley is not as deep or as wide as Waipio. Nevertheless, this verdant valley once sustained a sizable population, as evidenced by the stone walls and terraces that remain.

Waipio Valley, 3 miles to falls, 2 hours, (trail rating: strenuous).

The trailhead is at the pavilion, a 900-foot-high perch providing a striking panorama of Waipio

Valley. Your eye can easily follow the trail to Waimanu, which snakes up the northwest bluff and then into the valley, where numerous waterfalls drop into Waipio from the Kohala Mountains.

Carry as much water as you can, since safe drinking water is not available. Water in the valley irrigates farms and serves cattle which graze in the Kohala Mountains. To be on the safe side, use purification tablets or boil your water.

The paved jeep road drops an abrupt mile into the valley to a junction where one roads turns toward the beach and another into the valley. As you pause on your descent, look for yellow guava (Psidium guajava) within easy reach of the road.

Waipio Valley

The yellow, lemon-sized fruit is a tasty treat. The beach trail on the right passes some homesteads along Lalakea (a kind of shark) Fishpond on its way to the gray sand beach. It is common to find locals pushing and dragging their outriggers on Wailoa (lit., "long water") Stream to the open sea for a day of fishing. Note how they use the undulations of the surf to carry them over the rock-laden outlet, and conversely to beach their craft.

The thick, silky, green leaves of beach naupaka (Scaevola frutescens) greet the hiker on the beach. A common sight on most of Hawaii's beaches, the naupaka is a native variety that may grow to ten feet. It has a small, fragrant, white, half flower with small white berries following the flowers. There are several legends surrounding the naupaka flower. One claims that lovers were separated leaving half a flower, the young boy blooming alone in the mountains, and the other half flower, the girl, blossoming alone on the beach. If a whole flower is found on either the beach naupaka or the mountain naupaka, that means the couple have been united. Another legend recounts the story of the young prince who wished to marry a commoner. The king, the boy's father, interviewed the young woman inquiring as to her family background and to her virginity. On the latter concern, the king was skeptical so he charged his son and the girl to search the beach and the mountains for a whole flower on the naupaka, since it was the belief that a virgin could find a whole flower. Legend holds that the pair are still looking! Perhaps you can find one!

Camping in Waipio Valley is allowed on the east side of Waipio Stream by securing permission from the Davies Hamakua Sugar Co. Until 1977 the best and most popular campsites were on the west side of the stream among the trees that front the beach. This property is owned by the Bishop Museum of Honolulu, which closed the area to camping due to overcrowding. They have reported that they may allow camping in the future by permit only, limiting the number of campers. Ford Wailoa Stream where it enters the ocean and scout the

Waipio Valley stream crossing

beach for a picnic spot. The ironwood (Casuarina equisetifolia) trees that front the beach provide an umbrella from the hot sun and the rain. Also known as the Australian Pine, the ironwood has long, thin, drooping, dull-green needles whose droppings make a soft mat for a sleeping bag but are a fire danger. Approach ocean swimming with extreme caution: there is a strong surf with riptides.

To explore Waipio, return to the road junction and follow the road into the valley. You will be walking along the stream and toward Hiilawe (lit., "lift-carry") Falls. The falls may not be "turned on" since the stream that feeds it is used for irrigation and the water is frequently taken out above the falls. The road turns to cut across the valley. You pass the ruins of houses, the result of a devastating tidal wave, and some newly constructed homes. After fording several streams, you approach Nanaue Falls on the north side of the valley. The U.S. Peace Corps once trained here, but flooding in November 1979 destroyed the abandoned buildings that had served for training recruits who were going to serve in Asia.

Nanaue Falls can be reached by following the unpaved road to the shoreline and crossing Waipio Stream where it enters the ocean. Scout around for the safest place to cross. *Do not cross* if the stream is swollen or if the river is moving swiftly. Once across, follow the trail under the ironwood trees to the base of the cliff at the Waimanu trailhead (posted) and then walk south (left) on the trail to the falls. Remember that periodic flooding in Waipio destroys the trail and alters the flow of the stream so that the trail may be muddy and obscure. Nanaue is really a number of falls, some with generous swimming holes at their bases. Use CAUTION if you climb above the lowest fall. It is extremely wet and slippery.

There are numerous cardinals (Richmondena cardinalis) in the valley, which flush from the trees as you make your way. The male, with its all-red body and its pointed crest, and the black-and-red female were introduced from the mainland. Avocado, mountain apple, and yellow guava trees flourish in the valley, but respect the posted "kapu" (No Trespassing) signs. There are some trees as well as passion fruit vines along the road.

Waipio to Waimanu, 9 miles, 6 hours (trail rating: difficult).

The most difficult part of the trek to Waimanu is the ascent up the northwest pali (cliff) of Waipio Valley. The trail is easy to find about 100 yards from the beach in a forest at the base of the cliff. The switchbacks are steep but well-maintained. Obviously, this 1,200-foot climb is best approached in the cool of the morning.

From the ridge, the trail crosses 14 gulches to Waimanu; so it's up and down along the pali overlooking the rugged coastline. There are places where some rock slides make the going a bit difficult and slow, so be cautious. The trail is heavily forested and foliated and in some places overgrown. You're more likely to encounter horses than hikers on the trail since Waimanu is a popular pig hunting destination with locals. The trail shelter is nine gulches from Waipio Valley, or about two-thirds of the way to Waimanu. It is a satisfactory place to lunch or camp, although you may have to share it with other hikers.

As you swing out of Pukoa (lit., "coral head") Gulch, you get your first view of Waimanu Valley.

"Z" trail out of Waipio Valley

The similarity between Waipio and Waimanu will surprise you. Although Waimanu is about half the size of Waipio, it contains a similar verdant valley and is bounded by precipitous cliffs. It's a sight to behold.

Waimanu Stream greets you on the floor of the valley after a steep descent. The best place to ford Waimanu Stream is about 25 feet above the spot where the stream joins the ocean. For drinking water, hike about 1/2 mile along the west side of the pali to an unnamed waterfall. Once again, either treat the water or boil it before drinking. There are numerous beach-front camping sites, so scout around and find one that suits you. As at Waipio, beware of ocean swimming because of the heavy surf with riptides.

There are no trails here, since Waimanu, unlike Waipio, has long been abandoned. You will find stone walls and foundations as well as taro terraces remaining from when it was occupied.

The jewel of Waimanu is Waiilikahi (lit., "water with single surface") Falls, about 1 1/2 miles along the northwest pali of the valley. You must make your own trail to the falls. With luck, you'll arrive when the succulent mountain apples (Eugenia malaccensis) are ripe, usually in June. The fruit is a small red and pinkish apple with a thin waxy skin. Its white flesh is crisp and juicy. Enjoy your lunch, your apples, and a swim in the large pool below the falls.

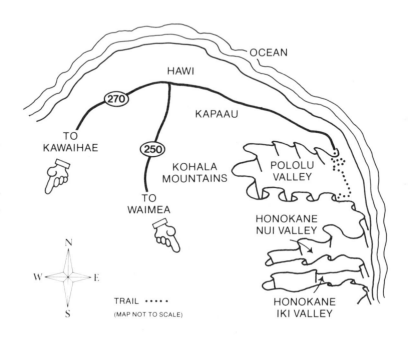

POLOLU VALLEY

(Hiking Area No. 8)

Rating: Strenuous.
Features: Native and introduced flora, swimming, views.
Permission: None.
Hiking Distance and time: 1/2 mile, 1/2 hour, 900-foot gain.

Driving Instructions:

From Hilo (80 miles, 2 hours) north on Route 19, right on Route 250, right on Route 270 to the end of the road.

From Kona (66 miles, 1 hour) north on Route 19, left on Route 270, to the end of the road.

Introductory Notes: Pololu (lit., "long spear") Valley is the trailhead for the Kohala ditch country and a 40-mile network of trails traversing the Kohala Mountains and beyond to Waimanu and Waipio valleys. The trail is not maintained, but is in fair condition since it is traversed by residents of Pololu. BE CAUTIOUS, particularly when the trail is wet and muddy. It can be very slippery and hazardous.

On the Trail: From the lookout at the end of the road, you get a good view of the beach below and the interior of the valley. If you have already been to Waipio and Waimanu, Pololu may seem a bit tame. The trail is a short one that drops 300 feet to the valley floor. Portions of the trail are eroded by rain, so be alert. Once on the floor of the valley, the trail turns into the valley, which is private land, and to the beach which is public. Walk along the beach, but beware of swimming, for the surf and riptides have taken a toll in human life in recent years. The best place to cross the stream is usually about 20-30 yards from the surf where the water is usually 3-4 feet deep. Once across the stream, you can follow the beach to the far end of the valley or walk into

Pali south of Pololu Valley

the ironwood trees at beach front where you will find the trail. Ironwood (Casuarina equisetifolia L.) is a leafless tree with long, thin, drooping, dull green needles and a cone resembling a pineapple. It is used largely as windbreak.

The trail in the trees is well-defined and in good condition. But as you ascend the pali (cliff) it is deeply rutted from rain. Fallen trees and heavy vegetation also make hiking difficult. However, you are rewarded for your efforts with marvelous views of the beachfront of Pololu Valley. You'll also find strawberry guava (Psidium cattleianum) here. It is a small tree (15 feet) with smooth bark and shiny, dark green leaves and white flowers. The fruit is red, golf-ball-sized and very tasty.

You're certain to find privacy and solitude in Pololu Valley and shady places to lunch. It's fun to search the beach for "treasure" swept ashore from passing or shipwrecked ships. Ocean swimming can be hazardous on the north and east sides of the islands. If you do so, be alert for swells and tide changes.

The trail beyond Pololu Beach is on private property and the owner will not grant permission to hike. A "NO TRESPASSING" sign is posted.

Let's swim!

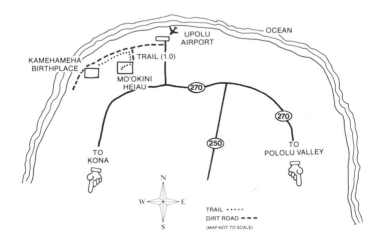

MO'OKINI LAUKINI HEIAU

(Hiking Area No. 9)

Rating: Family.
Features: Heiau (pre-Christian place of worship),
Kamehameha I birthplace/homesite.
Permission: None.
Hiking Distance and Time: 1 mile, 1 hour.
Driving Instructions:
From Hilo (81 miles, 2 hours) north on Route 19,
    right on Route 270, left on Upolu Airport Road

(2 miles) left on dirt road (1.7 miles) left at sign "Mo'okini Laukini" to end (0.2 mile).

From Kona (52 miles, 1 hour) north on Route 19, left on Route 270, then as above.

Introductory Notes: Mo'okini Laukini (lit., "many lineages"), a sacred heiau (a pre-Christian temple of worship), and King Kamehameha's birthplace nearby are two significant historical sites. This heiau was a "closed" religious place reserved for the alii nui (the kings and ruling chiefs) for fasting, praying and offering of human sacrifices to their gods. Therefore, commoners were not permitted inside the heiau until 1978 when Leimomi Mo'okini Lum, the present kahuna nui (priestess), lifted the kapu (taboo) that made it safe for the people to enter and to leave this sacred place. To some, the site and the remains of the heiau may not be impressive, but you should remember that it is a sacred place to others and should be respected. PLEASE DO NOT remove any stones or materials from the heiau.

On the Trail: Leave your auto outside the walls and pick up a pamphlet available at the entrance to the heiau that details the history and religious importance of Mo'okini Laukini. The following numbered highlights correspond to the numbers on the map.

1. Exterior wall built in 1981 to protect the site.

Mo'okini Heiau

2.   The guardian or god in the form of this rock is
     from the Kamehameha birthplace.
3.   Dish-shaped rock used by the priests to prepare
     victims for offering in the heiau.
4.   Furniture and implements used in ceremonies
     are made here.
5.   The House of the mu. The mu gathered
     sacrificial victims for religious offerings.
6.   Heiau entrance.

7. The alii nui enclosure was where the kings and ruling chiefs prayed, fasted and offered human sacrifices.
8. Priests' walkway to the altar.
9. The altar and focal point of the heiau.

According to the chants, Kamehameha the Great was born in 1758 nearby and was brought to the Mo'okini Laukini for his birth rituals.

To reach King Kamehameha's birthplace, walk down the road (0.2 mile) from the heiau, turn left at the junction and walk (0.3 mile) to the site. Kamehameha ("The Lonely One") was born here in 1758 (probable date) of parents of high rank, but not in direct line of kingly succession. He became a renowned warrior during his youth and by 1790 had won numerous battles. An oracle told him that if he wished to conquer Hawaii, he must build a large heiau at Puukohola, Kawaihae (see Hiking Area No. 11) in honor of the war god. The heiau was built and Keoua, Kamehamaha's major opponent for control of the island, was invited to the ceremony. As Keoua stepped ashore, he was slain by one of Kamehameha's chiefs. Thus did he gain sovereignty over Hawaii. During the next few years, he fought battles to secure control of the other islands and by 1795 he was master of all the islands except Kauai and Niihau, whose king acknowledged himself a subject of Kamehameha in 1810 after many years of fighting. Kamehameha the Great died in 1819.

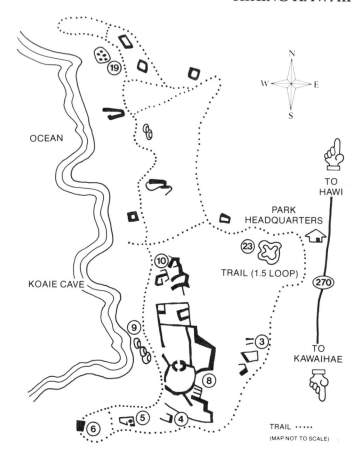

OCEAN

N
W   E
S

TO
HAWI

PARK
HEADQUARTERS

KOAIE CAVE

TRAIL (1.5 LOOP)

270

TO
KAWAIHAE

TRAIL ·····
(MAP NOT TO SCALE)

LAPAKAHI STATE HISTORICAL PARK

(Hiking Area No. 10)

Rating: Family.

Features: 600-year old Hawaiian Village (partly restored).
Permission: State Historical Park. No fee.
Hiking Distance and Time: 1.5 mile loop, 1 hour.
Driving Instructions:
From Hilo (80 miles, 2 hours) north on Route 19 to Kawaihae, right on Route 270 to park on beach side.
From Kona (47 miles, 1 hour) north on Route 19 to Kawaihae, left on Route 270 to park on beach side.

Introductory Notes: An easy hike into the past awaits the visitor at Lapakahi (lit., "single ridge"), where excavations continue to restore a bit of old Hawaii and to provide a lesson in sociology. Some 600 years ago fishermen moved into this ahupuaa (land division). They established a fishing village where they could easily launch their canoes, prepare their nets, dry their catch, and care for their ohana (family). They exchanged part of their catch with their friends and neighbors in the upland for fruits, vegetables and olona (Touchardia latifolia), a shrub from which nets and twine could be fashioned. It was truly a community of the makainana, or commoner. With the coming of the white man and the need for grazing land for his cattle, the people moved to other parts of the island.

On the Trail: The Park Service provides visitors with a free trail brochure that identifies 23 points of interest. The text below and the accompanying map make note of the highlights at this interesting and educational place.

From the visitor center and all along the trail, you have a good view of the surrounding countryside and the sea that sustained life at Lapakahi. Kiawe (Prosopis pallida) trees, with their gnarled trunks and fernlike leaves and thorny branches, dominate the landscape. They were an important source of fuel and lumber as well as medicine, tannin and honey.

#3 House and Burial Site. Prior to Western contact in 1778, a home stood on this site overlooking Koaie (a kind of tree) Village. Since the 19th century, the site has been used for burials.

#4 Canoe Shed. An important place in the village, where the valuable canoe could be stored, protected and repaired. The shape of the remaining walls in this halau (longhouse) makes it easy to imagine a canoe sheltered within.

#5 House site. Look for the two-by-four in one corner of the remains which suggests that it has been used as a dwelling in this century.

#6 Fish Shrine. To assure a good catch, offerings of food were made to the demigod Kuula by the fishermen. You will probably find some coins on this interestingly shaped rock. They were left by hopeful visitors.

Be certain to pause in the game area to test your skill at 'O'o ihe (spear throwing) and 'ulu maika (disk rolling). The former requires that you spear the

Lapakahi State Park

Fishing tools

banana stalk, and the latter is played by rolling the disk stone between the stakes. Players stand at opposite sides and roll the stones, receiving a point each time the stone rolls between the stakes.

#8 Water Well. The failure of such fresh-water wells may have caused the abandonment of Koaie Village.

#9 Salt Pans. Ocean water was poured into these stone pans and allowed to evaporate. As crystals formed, they were moved to shallower stones to dry, and then put into pans lined with ti leaves, in which the salt would be packaged for storage.

#10 Work and Storage Area. An activity center of the village where repairs to the nets and fishing equipment were made, and a storage area for fishing supplies.

#19 Papamu (game board). Konane, or Hawaiian checkers, was a very popular game in ancient Hawaii. It is played on a papamu stone with black and white playing stones that are placed in the depressions. The game requires two players and is not unlike checkers in that players may jump each other's stones provided there is a space between. The game is won by taking all the opponent's stones.

#23 Shelters. These "guest" shelters were used by visiting relatives and friends.

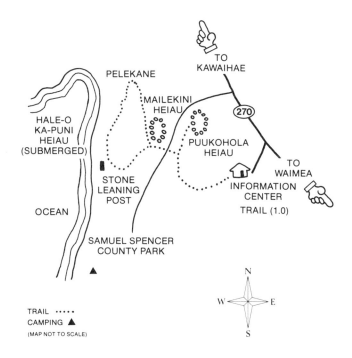

TRAIL ·····
CAMPING ▲
(MAP NOT TO SCALE)

PUUKOHOLA HEIAU

(Hiking Area No. 11)

Rating: Hardy family.

Features: Pre-Christian place of worship; historical site.

Permission: National Historic Site. No fee.

Hiking Distance and Time: 1 mile, 1 hour.

Driving Instructions:

From Hilo (63 miles, 1 1/2 hours) north on Route 19, right on Route 270, left at Park Entrance.

From Kona (35 miles, 1 hour) north on Route 19, left on Route 270, left at Park Entrance.

Introductory Notes: Archeological work continues at Puukohola Heiau, established as a national historic site in 1972. Some of the park is inaccessible unless you are a skin diver! Hale-O-Ka-Puni Heiau, dedicated to the shark gods, is believed to be under water just off the coastline. Nevertheless, a good foot trail takes you to the remains of this once-active community.

Heiaus (pre-Christian places of worship) played an important part in the cultural and religious life of the early Hawaiians. There are hundreds of known heiaus on the island. Some served specifically to insure rain, good crops, or success in war, while others were used for human sacrifice.

Puukohola Heiau

Kamehameha I had Puukohola (lit., "hill of the whale") Heiau constructed in 1790-91 in hopes of fulfilling a prophecy that if he did so, he would become the ruler of all the islands. As king of the northwest part of Hawaii, he had been unsuccessfully fighting his neighboring chieftains. The famous prophet Kapoukahi told Kamehameha's aunt that Kamehameha would conquer the islands if he built a large temple to his family war god Kukailimoku above the village of Kawaihae (lit., "the water of wrath"). Work commenced in 1790 while war raged, and the heiau was completed in the summer of 1791. Kamehameha invited his rival Keoua Kuahuula to the dedication to make peace. As soon as Kuahuula stepped ashore, however, he was killed and his body carried to the heiau and offered as the principal sacrifice to Kamehameha's war god. With Kuahuula's death, opposition on Hawaii ended. In 1794 Kamehameha conquered the islands of Maui, Lanai and Molokai, and in 1795, Oahu. When Kauai's king consented to Kamehameha's rule in 1810, the prophecy was fulfilled.

On the Trail: The trail begins at the information center. However, if you are camping at Spencer County Park, it is a short walk up the road to the trail at the base of Puukohola Heiau. (The feature numbers below are from a government map.)

#1 The Heiau that Kamehameha Built - Puukohola. The heiau is an imposing structure when viewed from the road. Imagine the 224 x 100 foot platform covered with wooden images of Hawaiian gods, houses, a prayer tower, an altar, and other temple furnishings. After Kamehameha's death in 1819, the heiau was abandoned and all the trappings were moved, destroyed or left to decay.

#2 Mailekini (lit., "many maile vines") Heiau. This heiau, erected to the war gods of Kamehameha's ancestors, was reputed by early English missionaries to be nearly equal to Puukohola in size. It also served as a fort to protect Kawaihae Village.

#3 Hale-O-Ka-Puni Heiau. The exact location of Hale-O-Ka-Puni (lit., "house of Kapuni" - a high priest) is not known. Although it was covered by the sea, records indicate that it did exist and was dedicated to the shark gods.

#4 The Stone Leaning Post. It is here that the high chief, Alapai-Kupalupalu-mano, rested as he watched the sharks circle Hale-O-Ka-Puni before they devoured the offerings he had placed there.

#5 Pelekane. Pelekane is the site of the royal residence.

#6 John Young's House. Little remains of the home of this British sailor who became a trusted adviser to Kamehameha the Great, married his niece, served as governor of the island of Hawaii, and was business agent for the king. It is believed that one of his homes here was constructed of stone and mortar — the first western-type house on the islands.

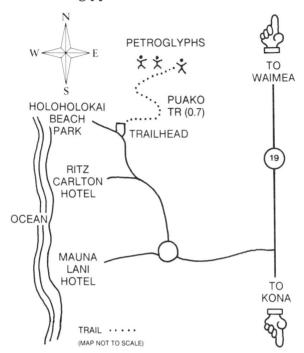

PUAKO PETROGLYPHS

(Hiking Area No. 12)

Rating: Family.
Features: Hawaiian petroglyphs.
Permission: None.
Hiking Distance and Time: 0.7 mile, 1/2 hour.
Driving Instructions:
From Hilo (74 miles, 2 hours) north on Route 19,
    right for 2.4 miles on road to Mauna Lani

Hotel/Ritz Carlton Hotel, bear right following signs to Puako Petroglyphs/Holoholokai Beach park.

From Kona (29 miles, 1 hour) north on Route 19, left for 2.4 miles on road to Mauna Lani Hotel/Ritz Carlton Hotel, then as above.

Introductory Notes: Petroglyphs are drawings or carvings on rock made by prehistoric or primitive people. Those at Puako (lit., "sugar cane blossom"), of unknown origin, are some of the finest examples on the islands, and probably the most numerous.

On the Trail: Several interpretive signs and displays are found at the trailhead. The trail to the petroglyphs is initially paved, but soon becomes a well-defined dirt path that twists and turns through a kiawe tree forest. The wood of this tree is a source not only of fuel and lumber but also of honey, medicine, tannin and fodder, which is produced from its beanlike yellow pods. It's a hot and dusty walk to the petroglyphs. All the drawings and carvings are on pahoehoe lava, which has a smooth or ropy surface. While the meanings of some are obvious, others challenge the imagination. It is almost like browsing in a bookstore or in an antique store. You are irresistibly drawn to look and look and look. To some, petroglyphs are the art of past civilizations and have sophisticated meanings. To others, they are the casual scribbles of an illiterate people — just old graffiti. What do you think?

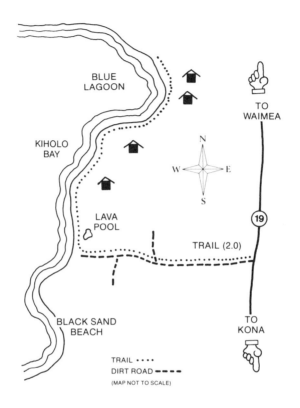

KIHOLO BAY

(Hiking Area No. 13)

Rating: Hardy Family.
Features: Swimming (blue lagoon), tidepools.
Permission: None.
Hiking Distance and Time: 2 miles, 1 hour.

Driving Instructions:

From Hilo (87 miles, 2 hours) north on Route 19 (to Kailua-Kona) to 82.5 mile marker past lookout, right on paved road/gate/parking.

From Kona (17 miles, 1/2 hour) north on Route 19, then as above.

Introductory Notes: Kiholo (lit., "fish hook") Bay is an easy hike to an uncrowded coastline and to a gentle, peaceful, blue-water lagoon. Even if the access road off the highway to the beach is unguarded and unlocked, I suggest you leave your vehicle outside the gate. The gate may be locked when you return.

On the Trail: The trailhead, just off the highway, provides parking space. The trail (a rough, unpaved jeep road) descends gradually to the beach. You're certain to sight numerous mynah (Acridotheres tristis) birds which are found on all the main islands at lower elevations. This amusing (it walks as well as hops) little bird with a black head, yellow coloring around the eye and yellow bill, has white wing patches when in flight. Cardinals and doves are also abundant here. "Hawaii's Birds," published by the Audubon Society, is a helpful and valuable book if you wish to learn and to identify native and introduced birds.

Near the coastline, you'll reach a large open area and a path (left side) that passes through the trees to the beach. (You should mark this place so that you will readily locate it on your return). From here, you are left of center of Kiholo Bay. To the left about 150 yards is located a black sand beach suitable for swimming and to the right, at the far end of the bay, lies a beautiful blue lagoon. Look for a small, water-filled crack/hole in the lava on the right about 100 yards north from the point where you reached the coast. Some hikers like to sit in the cool, brackish water to cleanse after swimming in the salty ocean. I don't. Too many people have trashed the area and it's not clean.

Continuing along the shoreline, you'll see several homesites scattered among the trees. Most appear to be weekend retreats since the beach is deserted on weekdays. The lagoon is at the far end of the bay, but you'll know when you arrive. Wow! The aquamarine water is in stark contrast to the white sand beaches intruded by black lava. It's a delightful place to picnic, swim and to find a large measure of solitude.

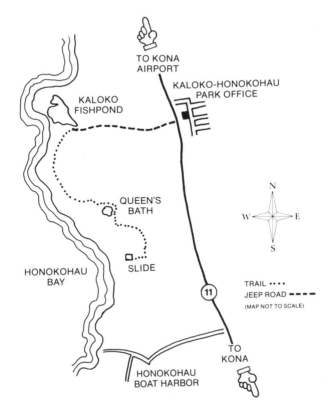

KALOKO-HONOKOHAU NATIONAL HISTORICAL PARK

(Hiking Area No. 14)

Rating: Hardy Family.
Features: Queen's bath, holua (ancient slide), tide-pools, swimming.

Permission: None.
Hiking Distance and Time: 2 miles, 1 hour.
Driving Instructions:
From Hilo (100 miles, 2 1/2 hours) north on Route
19 (to Kailua-Kona) right on unpaved jeep road
opposite Kona Trade Center to end.
From Kona (4 miles, 15 minutes) north on Route
19, left on unpaved jeep road opposite Kona
Trade Center to end.

Introductory Notes: Kaloko-Honokohau
(Kaloko, lit., "the pond" and Honokohau, lit., "adze
bay") National Historic Park was established by
Congress in 1978 to preserve native Hawaiian ac-
tivities and culture and to demonstrate historic land
use patterns. According to Francis Kuailani, acting
superintendent, the park includes large Hawaiian
fishponds, house sites, a heiau, petroglyphs, graves,
and native and migrant water birds. He told me that
the park is not yet operational and only the northern
portion, Kaloko, is open to the public. He concluded
that the government is hoping to purchase the land
where Queen's bath and the holua (slide) are located.

On the Trail: Rangers and park personnel who
may be present at the trailhead are the best source of
information regarding the preserve, and they love to
"talk story." Facing the ocean, Koloko Pond is on
the right and the trail (jeep road) goes left from the
front of the ranger's trailer and follows the coastline. Morning glory flowers and beach naupaka

Queen's Bath

(Scaevola taccada) dominate the trailside. The latter is a spreading succulent shrub with white berries and small white, half-flowers. One version of a Polynesian legend holds that lovers were separated leaving a half flower of the girl blossoming alone on the beach and her sweetheart blooming alone in the mountains on the mountain naupaka, a relative of the beach variety.

After approximately one-fourth mile the trail turns away from the beach, leaves park land, and requires the hiker to duck — nearly crawl — under the interlocking branches of the hau tree where it emerges on a lava field. The hau (Hibiscus tiliaceus) a true hibiscus, bears bright yellow flowers with a dark center. During the day the flower turns to apricot color and to deep red before it falls.

The trail across the lava field to Queen's bath is relatively clear to follow as it turns in the direction of the highway and toward ten piles or mounds of lava rock that encircle the bath. It is believed that Queen Kaahumanu, King Kamehameha's favorite wife, bathed here while the king's guards stood atop the lava mounds to ensure her privacy. The bath is quite small, about 30 feet in circumference, 3 feet deep in the deepest part, and is surprisingly cool. Although it does not appeal to me, you may choose to splash or to sit in the bath.

From Queen's bath the trail goes south, paralleling the beach on the right and the highway on the left and passes between two large lava piles, and turns left in the direction of the highway. The trail becomes obscure as you cross the aa (rough, clinkery type) lava. To reach the holua (sled) loop around the brush and trees on your right and head for the higher lava flows to the southeast. Don't be discouraged if you cannot find the trail, but be CAUTIOUS walking on the rough underfooting. IT'S HAZARDOUS and razor sharp.

There is no mistaking the holua; it's a large, 15-by-100-foot, long incline that some believe was much larger when first constructed since it probably reached the water or pond enabling fun seekers to end their ride in the water. There are many known slides on the islands since contests were very popular with the royalty and with the people. The surface of the slide was usually covered with mud and pili grass to provide a smooth surface. The papa (sled) was constructed from wood. Some were 8-9 feet long with runners no more than six inches apart. In competition, sledders could reach 30 to 60 miles per hour, and some were known to ride the sled as a surfer rides a board.

Instead of retracing your steps to the trailhead, you could walk south a short distance to a dirt road that leads to the beach where you can find places to cool off, and then return to your transportation by following the coastline north.

Holua — sled

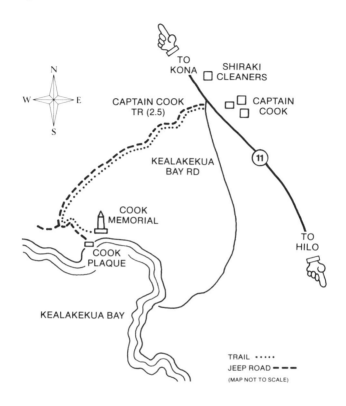

CAPTAIN COOK MONUMENT

(Hiking Area No. 15)

Rating: Strenuous.
Features: Site of Captain Cook's death, mango, papaya, avocado, guava, ancient Hawaiian burial caves, swimming, snorkeling.
Permission: None.
Hiking Distance and Time: 2.5 miles, 2 hours.

Driving Instructions:

From Hilo (113 miles, 3 hours) south on Route 11 to Captain Cook, sharp left just past Captain Cook on Bay Road, opposite a cleaning business, and drive one-tenth mile to jeep road (trail) on the right.

From Kona (14 miles, 1/2 hour) south on Route 11 to Captain Cook, and same as above.

Introductory Notes: This is my favorite hike on the island. It is a delightful trek with a generous supply of nature's best fruits to suit anyone's palate.

The trailhead is a bit difficult to find. Look for a dry cleaners on the main road just north of the town of Captain Cook. Almost opposite the store, the road to Kealakekua (lit.,"pathway of the god") Bay drops abruptly to the left. The trail itself begins about 500 feet down this road. It is a jeep road, on the corner of which is a large avocado tree. Find the trail, for the hike is worth the effort. You should carry a small daypack to load up on fruits along the first 1/2 mile. Mango (Mangifera indica) is particularly abundant in the fields and along the roadside. Look under the trees for those that have fallen and are not too badly bruised, or find a stick to shake some loose from the trees. If you find a good long stick, leave it near the trail for the next hiker.

One of the favorite fruits of visitors and locals is the papaya (Carica papaya). The ripe yellow fruit varies in size, but can be found growing in clusters

Where's the trail?

at the bases of umbrella-like leaves. In ancient Hawaii, the leaves were used as soap and as a meat tenderizer, and the seeds were used medicinally. You will find numerous papaya trees along the roadside.

As if this weren't enough, there are also some avocado (Persea americana) trees. Their fruit tends to be too watery for some people's taste, but perhaps not for yours.

On The Trail: From the trailhead, the trail/jeep road descends about 50 yards to where the road turns right into private property, and your trail goes left into tall — 6 to 8 foot — grass. In July, 1989, the trail was not marked or posted and the trail was indistinguishable. On the other hand the trail goes straight to the coast, paralleling a stone wall on the left. The trail is heavily overgrown for the first mile, but then opens as you near the coast. Here, the terrain becomes more arid, sustaining only low scrub. You have your first view of the coast, a portion of Kealakekua Bay, and your destination, although the Cook Memorial is hidden in the trees. Bear left toward the beach at the first junction in the road. From here, go straight on to the beach. When you reach the beach, follow the coast to the left for a few hundred feet to the memorial. You needn't be concerned about the tourist boats' disturbing your visit, for the passengers do not disembark. The boats simply make a pass by the memorial and anchor in the bay for people who wish to snorkel for a short time. You will find that snorkeling is outstanding here.

There are numerous caves beyond the monument and along the walls of the cliff. If you choose to explore, do not disturb any interesting finds. A number of local people are seeking the preserve what may be ancient Hawaiian burial grounds.

Captain Cook was killed here at water's edge on February 14, 1779 by the Hawaiians. Cook, an English captain in the employ of the Earl of Sandwich, was in search of a northwest passage when he sighted and landed on the Hawaiian Islands (he named them the Sandwich Islands after his benefactor) in 1778 where he supplied his ships. He was thought to be the god Lono who was revered by the natives, so that he and his men were treated well. Cook returned a year later, January 1779, and anchored in Kealakekua Bay where he was warmly greeted again by thousands (estimates range from 30,000 to 50,000 Hawaiians). For a month the haoles (foreigners) were given a bounty of food and supplies to a point that the native people were deprived. This angered some of the people and Cook wisely left on February 4. He was compelled to return a week later since one of his ships was in need of repair and since storms on the north part of the island forced Cook to seek calmer waters. He again anchored in Kealakekua Bay on February 11. The Hawaiians, who on Cook's previous visit had "borrowed" or "used" or "stolen" items from the ship, "took" a cutter (small boat) from one of the ships. When the captain learned of the matter, he was enraged and with a number of armed marines went to shore to retrieve the boat. Meanwhile, the natives armed themselves and the opposing forces met on the beach. A fight resulted between a few natives and marines and, as Cook turned his back to the Hawaiians (some believe he tried to stop his men), he was struck in the head and he fell. Daggers were drawn and Cook was repeatedly stabbed by numerous natives. The result was that Cook and four marines were killed as well as an indeterminate number of natives. Some historians believe that the Hawaiians engaged in cannibalism, but there is insufficient evidence of this occurring. It does seem certain that the natives stripped his flesh from the bones (a traditional Hawaiian practice reserved for kings) and hid the bones where they could not be found. An unfortunate end for all.

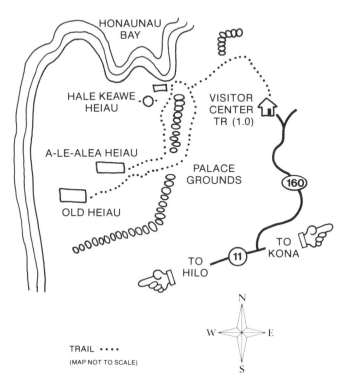

HONAUNAU
BAY

HALE KEAWE
HEIAU

VISITOR
CENTER
TR (1.0)

A-LE-ALEA HEIAU

PALACE
GROUNDS

160

OLD HEIAU

TO
KONA

TO
HILO

11

N

W ← → E

S

TRAIL ••••
(MAP NOT TO SCALE)

CITY OF REFUGE

(Hiking Area No. 16)

Rating: Family.
Features: City of Refuge, National Historic Sites.
Permission: Admission fee.
Hiking Distance and Time: 1 mile, 1 hour.

Driving Instructions:

From Hilo (111 miles, 3 hours) south on Route 11,
    left on Route 160 to City of Refuge.

From Kona (20 miles, 3/4 hour) south on Route 11,
    right on Route 160 to City of Refuge.

Introductory Notes: There were two ways to
survive a war in old Hawaii. Either you defeated
your enemy or you sought the protection of a place
of refuge. War refugees were purified by the priests,
and eventually freed to return home in peace, protected from retribution. Kapu (a system of taboos)
breakers were similarly treated. The refuge at
Honaunau (Puuhonua-o-Honaunau) is only one of

City of Refuge Wall

many on the islands, but is the most important since it remains almost intact.

This city of refuge was divided into three sections. Within the great wall (Puuhonua section) the priests administered to the needs of the women, the children, the aged and the maimed as well as the defeated warriors and kapu breakers who were fleeing battle or were seeking absolution for their wrongdoings. Outside the wall were the palace grounds, which were taboo to all but the chiefs, the royal family, and the palace guard. For a commoner to walk on these grounds or even to cast a shadow on them was punishable by death. The third section, across the bay, was where the common people lived and worked.

A hike through this place of refuge is truly a walk into the past. Many lessons of Hawaiian society and culture are here.

On the Trail: The sights and sounds of old Hawaii introduce you to the city of refuge as you begin your hike to the recorded sounds of the Kumulipo (creation chant) and the sight of the tile murals at the trailhead. Take a moment to listen to the tape messages before you enter the palace grounds. They set the mood for an understanding of and a feeling for Hawaiian pre-Christian culture.

The palace grounds were the traditional seat of the kingdom of Kona (lit., "leeward"), where the king ruled in a large one-room structure of wooden frame work covered with thatch. The king might

Konane (checkers)

have had as many as 10 of these homes, each serv-
ing a specific purpose. Imagine royalty fishing in the
pond that was reserved for the chiefs or playing
Hawaiian "checkers" (konane) on the stone spe-
cially made for that purpose. And at Keoneele Cove,
picture the royal canoe being beached, or royalty
splashing and swimming in the warm, still water.

The great wall separating the palace grounds
from the puuhonua (sanctuary) was built by the
chief Keawe-ku-i-ke-kaai about 1550 A.D. The
wall, averaging 10 feet in height and about 17 feet
in width, was constructed using traditional Hawaiian
dry-wall masonry, whereby stones were fitted together without mortar. One of the largest stones is 6
1/2 feet high, 5 feet wide, and 2 feet thick, and

weighs 4-6 tons. Legend holds that the wall has a number of secret passageways, but some of the hollow interiors were created merely to save time and materials in building.

Hale-O-Keawe (lit., "house of Keawe") Heiau is probably the most photographed temple on the island. It served as the royal mausoleum, where the bones of 23 chiefs were housed. It was believed that these bones contained mana (spiritual power) that served to further protect the place of refuge. The flora in the area made an important contribution to the community. The hala (Pandanus odoratissimus), with its long, narrow, pointed leaves, was woven into mats, sails, pillows and sandals, while the fruit was strung into leis. The milo (Thespesia populnea) tree was used to produce bowls, other vessels and calabashes. It is an upright tree with heart-shaped leaves and yellow flowers that resemble hibiscus blossoms. And, of course, there is the ever-present coconut (Cocos nucifera) tree, which provided food and oil. Cord, mats, and brushes were made from the husk, baskets and fans from the leaves, and spears, posts and drums from the trunk.

Periodically, local Hawaiians are sponsored by the Park Service to showcase their skills in a variety of arts and crafts, from basket-weaving, mat-weaving and hat-weaving to pounding poi and making leis. It certainly will add a dimension to your visit if they are so employed when you are there.

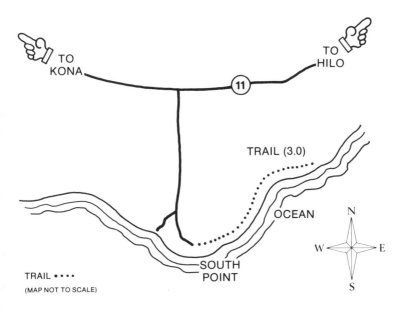

TO
KONA

TO
HILO

11

TRAIL (3.0)

OCEAN

N

W   E

S

SOUTH
POINT

TRAIL • • • •
(MAP NOT TO SCALE)

SOUTH POINT

(Hiking Area No. 17)

Rating: Hardy Family.
Features: Green-sand beach, swimming, beach-combing.
Permission: None.
Hiking Distance and Time: 3 miles, 1 hour.

Driving Instructions:
From Hilo (80 miles, 2 hours) south on Route 11, left at sign "South Point" to end (bear left at junction near the coast) to small boat harbor.
From Kona (64 miles, 1 1/2 hours) south on Route 11, right at sign "South Point" then as above.

Introductory Notes: Ke Lae or South Point is the southernmost point in the United States, the site of one of the oldest known Hawaiian settlements (about 750 A.D.) and the place where you can relax on a green sand beach. You should carry an ice chest with drinks, water, and food since there are no services available.

The 11-mile, narrow, bumpy road off Route 11 to South Point offers noteworthy points of interest. The whirring sound of numerous wind generators — too many to count— intrudes on the solitude about midpoint along the road.

Turn right at the junction, just before reaching the coastline, and you'll reach an automated lighthouse at road's end. Kalalea (lit., "prominent") Heiau, a pre-Christian place of worship, stands here. Even today, some fishermen make offerings of food to the mana (spirit). The heiau is believed to hold a shark or other god over which prayers are repeated.

Bear left at the junction and you are one mile from a small boat harbor and the trailhead. You will have passed through an abandoned WW II military base and airport before reaching the starting point.

On the Trail: Your trail is a jeep road that snakes along the rugged coastline for many miles. You'll find numerous jeep roads that crisscross here. Some roads lead to the shoreline where you're likely to find locals casting for a meal while other roads lead upcountry to grazing land. Choose the road paralleling the coast that provides the best underfooting although you may opt to follow the beach in hopes of finding "treasure" (junk?) swept ashore from passing or shipwrecked ships. In any event the variety of "stuff" here is a beachcomber's delight.

The area is dominated by low grass so that your view upland and along the coast is unobstructed. The only distractions here are the sound of the ocean and sight of grasshoppers leaping from the ground usually a footstep away. At midpoint, your destination is visible. Look for a black-sand promontory rising above water's edge about one and one-half miles distant. The green sand beach is at the base of the hill.

There is no mistaking the green sand beach. Yes, it is most definitely green. The sand is largely olivine crystals, a semiprecious stone. Use CAUTION when you descend to the beach and if you swim in the water here. It's a choice spot to lunch, swim and relax.

MAUNA KEA SUMMIT
(Hiking Area No. 18)

Rating: Difficult.

Features: Highest point on Hawaii, 13,796 feet.

Permission: Permits for state cabins and/or access road to Hale Pohaku: Dept. of Land & Natural Resources.

Hiking Distance and Time: 6 miles, 8-10 hours.

Driving Instructions:

From Hilo (35 miles, 1 hour) west on Route 200, right at Humuula Junction to Hale Pohaku (9,620 feet).

From Kona (62 miles, 2 hours) north on Route 190, right on Route 200, left at Humuula Junction to Hale Pohuka (9,620 feet).

Introductory Notes: The hike to Hawaii's highest point (13,796) is not as difficult as it might appear at first glance. There are both a hiking trail and a jeep trail to the summit and to the observatory. Indeed, in an ordinary passenger car it is possible to drive to the 9,620 foot level, and farther in a four-wheel-drive vehicle. You should make your ascent and descent in one day because no camping is permitted and there are no trail shelters or cabins. Begin your ascent early in the morning while it is still cool at lower elevations. Since snow is common at higher elevations, with temperatures dipping to 15 degrees Fahrenheit in winter, dress warmly even

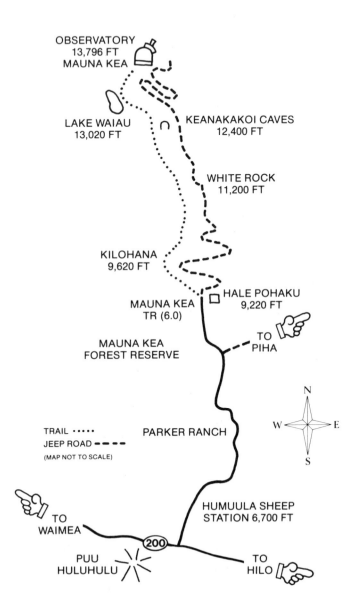

OBSERVATORY
13,796 FT
MAUNA KEA

LAKE WAIAU
13,020 FT

KEANAKAKOI CAVES
12,400 FT

WHITE ROCK
11,200 FT

KILOHANA
9,620 FT

MAUNA KEA
TR (6.0)

HALE POHAKU
9,220 FT

TO
PIHA

MAUNA KEA
FOREST RESERVE

N

W   E

S

TRAIL •••••
JEEP ROAD ▬ ▬ ▬
(MAP NOT TO SCALE)

PARKER RANCH

TO
WAIMEA

HUMUULA SHEEP
STATION 6,700 FT

200

PUU
HULUHULU

TO
HILO

in summer and wear sound hiking boots. Remember, if you are going to drive to the 9,620 foot level you must contact the Division of State Parks for permission and for a key to the gate.

On the Trail: From the trailhead at Hale Pohaku (lit., "stone house") the foot trail ascends northwestward and the jeep road northeastward. Since the cinder jeep road is firmer and more gradually sloped than the foot trail, you may choose to take it to the summit and return via the foot path. The trail is well-defined by steel posts and ahus (stone cairns).

You may see a number of birds common to this area. Be on the lookout for the large (three-foot-long) ring-necked pheasant (Phasianus colchicus torquatus) and the smaller chukar (Alectoris graeca), with its brownish-black markings and a black band extending through each eye and joining at the lower throat. Californians should recognize the common California quail (Lophortyx californicus), with its striking black plume and its bluish-gray breast and brown backing.

As you ascend, look south for startling views of the saddle (the area between Mauna Kea and Mauna Loa) and of Mauna Loa beyond. The altitude and the gradient will test your lungs and legs, and stops will be frequent. The first couple of miles are steep and difficult, until you reach "White Rock," a large outcropping of rock painted white, located at 11,200 feet.

The trail from here to Lake Waiau (lit., "swirling water") (13,020 feet) is considerably easier. At the 12,000-foot level, be on the lookout for a trail that leads to the Keanakakoi (lit., "cave of the adzes") Caves, where ancient Hawaiians mined the stones for their adzes. It is a National Historic Landmark and the world's most extensive ancient adze quarry. It is a short 1/4 mile from the jeep road.

At Lake Waiau, you are about 700 feet from the summit. The lake, 400 feet across and 15 feet deep, is a rather remarkable phenomenon, since an impervious bottom in an otherwise porous lava area keeps the water from seeping away. This the highest lake in the United States.

The summit of Mauna Kea (lit., "white mountain") is a cluster of cones from which Haleakala on the island of Maui may be visible to the northwest. The observatory here is operated by the University of Hawaii in cooperation with the U.S. Air Force and NASA

Appendix

Superintendent
Hawaii Volcanoes Nat'l Park
Hawaii, 96718
☎ (808) 967-7311

- park information
- hiking permits
- camping permits, where applicable

Volcano House
Hawaii Volcanoes Nat'l Park
Hawaii, 96718
☎ (808) 967-7321

- rental camper cabins at Namakani Paio
- hotel rooms at Volcano House

Dept. of Parks and Rec.
County of Hawaii
25 Aupuni Street
Hilo, HI 96720
☎ (808) 961-8311

- camping permits for county parks

Division of State Parks
State of Hawaii
P.O. Box 936
75 Aupuni Street
Hilo, HI 96720
☎ (808) 961-7200

- camping permits for state parks
- rental cabin information and permits
- hunting and fishing requirements

Hawaii County Transit System
25 Aupuni Street
Hilo, HI 96720
☎ (808) 935-8241

- bus information and schedules

Hawaii Visitor's Bureau
180 Kinoole Street
Hilo, HI 96720
☎ (808) 961-5797
or
75-5719 W. Alii Drive
Kailua-Kona, HI 96740
☎ (808) 329-7787

- general information

INDEX

ORDER FORM

HIKING KAUAI	$9.95
HIKING MAUI	$9.95
HIKING HAWAII	$9.95
HAWAII'S BEST HIKING TRAILS	$12.95

FORWARD TO:

NAME: _____

ADDRESS: _____

CITY: _____ STATE: _____ ZIP: _____

QUANTITY		PRICE		TOTAL
____	HIKING KAUAI	@ $9.95	=	
____	HIKING MAUI	@ $9.95	=	
____	HIKING HAWAII	@ $9.95	=	
____	HAWAII'S BEST HIKING TRAILS	@ $12.95	=	
	CA residents add 7¾% sales tax per book		=	
	Postage/Handling (Book rate)		=	$1.50
	(Free postage/handling for order of 2 or more books)			_____
	TOTAL ENCLOSED		=	____

MAIL TO:

Hawaiian Outdoor Adventures
P.O. Box 869
Huntington Beach, CA 92648